Young Louis XIV

Also by Burke Wilkinson

Novels

PROCEED AT WILL

RUN, MONGOOSE

LAST CLEAR CHANCE

(published as the trilogy *The Adventures of Goeffrey Mildmay*)

NIGHT OF THE SHORT KNIVES

Navy Stories

BY SEA AND BY STEALTH

French History for Younger Readers

THE HELMET OF NAVARRE

CARDINAL IN ARMOR

YOUNG LOUIS XIV

Espionage Anthology

CRY SPY!

Young

Louis XIV

The Early Years of the Sun King

by BURKE WILKINSON

illustrated by Doreen Roberts

The Macmillan Company

FOR EILEEN
with love

The Macmillan Company
866 Third Avenue
New York, New York 10022
Collier-Macmillan Canada, Ltd., Toronto, Ontario
Library of Congress catalog card number: 70-89596
Printed in the United States of America
FIRST PRINTING

CONTENTS

PART I

The Early Years

1. A Dauphin for France 3
2. A Wintry King, a Giddy Queen 6
3. Time of Change 10
4. The Mighty Victory 15
5. The Rise of Giulio Mazarini 22
6. A Solemn Childhood 28
7. Regency Honeymoon 33
8. France on Two Brinks 37

PART II

The Years of Tumult

9. The Slingshot Time 45
10. Flight by Starlight 52
11. Breastplates and Violins 56
12. The Fronde of the Princes 62
13. Of Codes and Cavalcades 69

14. Cannons on the Causeway 75
15. The Fronde in Frenzy 80

PART III

The Sun Goes Up the Sky

16. The Legend of the Divine Dove 89
17. Apprentice King 96
18. Some Anxious Months 103
19. The Island in the River 111
20. Death of a Cardinal 119
21. "How High Will I Not Climb?" 123
22. Supper Chez Fouquet 129
23. The Fall of the Squirrel 134

Epiloque 140
Chronology 142
Bibliography 143
Index 145

PRINCIPAL CHARACTERS

The Royal Family

LOUIS XIV (1638–1715)
LOUIS XIII, his father (died 1643)
ANNE OF AUSTRIA, his mother, the Queen Regent
PHILIP, DUC D'ANJOU, his brother
GASTON D'ORLEANS ("Monsieur"), his uncle
ANNE DE MONTPENSIER ("The Great Mademoiselle"), Gaston's daughter

The Military Leaders

LOUIS DE BOURBON, known as the Great Condé
HENRI DE LA TOUR D'AUVERGNE, Vicomte de Turenne

The Prime Ministers

ARMAND, CARDINAL RICHELIEU (died 1642)
JULES, CARDINAL MAZARIN

The Troublemakers

PAUL DE GONDI, CARDINAL DE RETZ
THE DUCHESSE DE LONGUEVILLE, sister of the Great Condé
THE PRINCE DE CONTI, his brother
NICHOLAS FOUQUET, Superintendent of Finance

The Ladies

MARIE MANCINI, Louis XIV's first love
MARIA THERESA, INFANTA OF SPAIN, his first wife
LOUISE DE LA VALLIÈRE, his first mistress

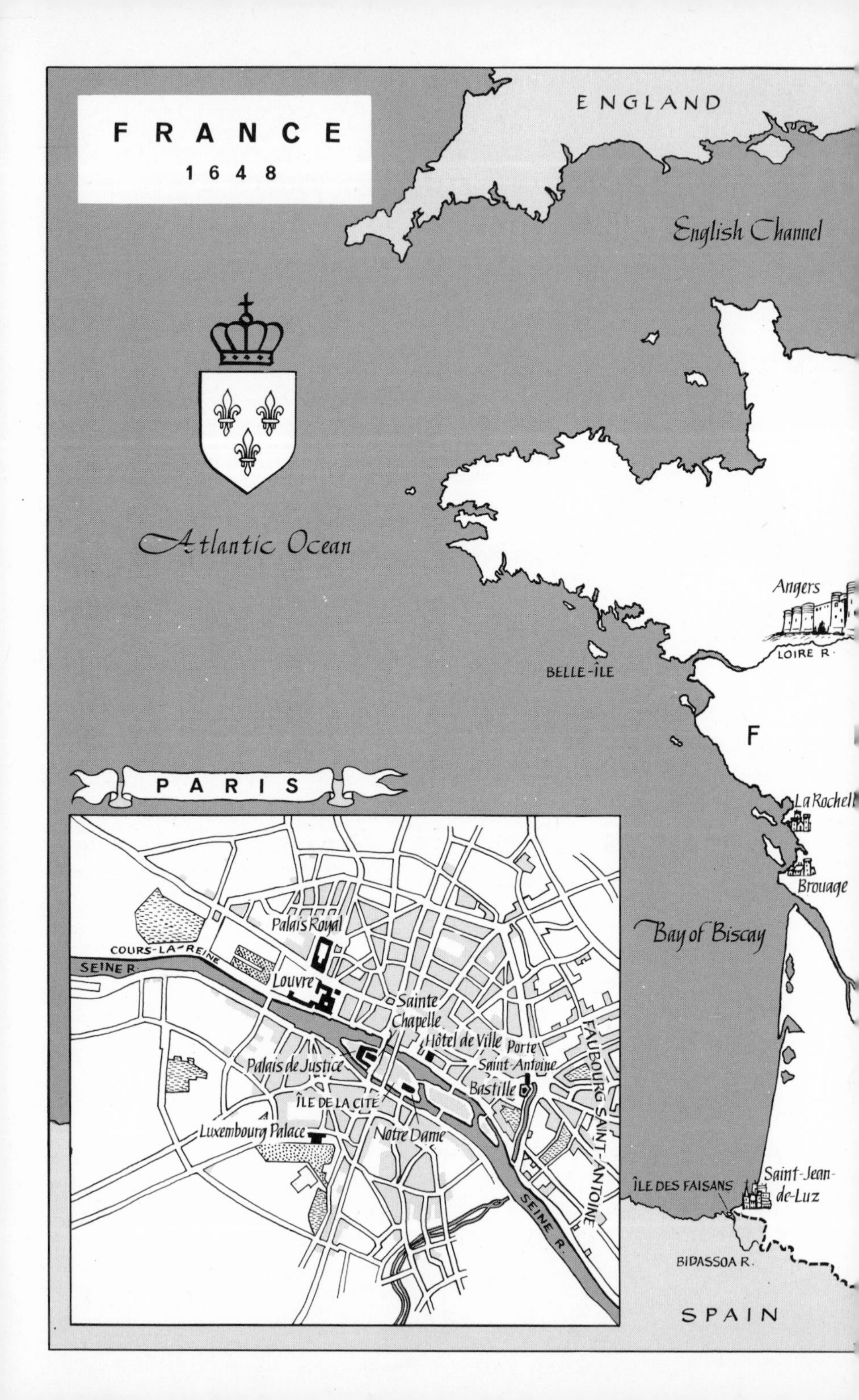
FRANCE
1648
ENGLAND
English Channel
Atlantic Ocean
Angers
LOIRE R.
BELLE-ÎLE
F
La Rochell
Brouage
Bay of Biscay
ÎLE DES FAISANS
Saint-Jean-de-Luz
BIDASSOA R.
SPAIN
PARIS
Palais Royal
COURS-LA-REINE
SEINE R.
Louvre
Sainte Chapelle
Hôtel de Ville
Porte Saint-Antoine
Palais de Justice
Bastille
ÎLE DE LA CITÉ
Luxembourg Palace
Notre Dame
FAUBOURG SAINT-ANTOINE
SEINE R.

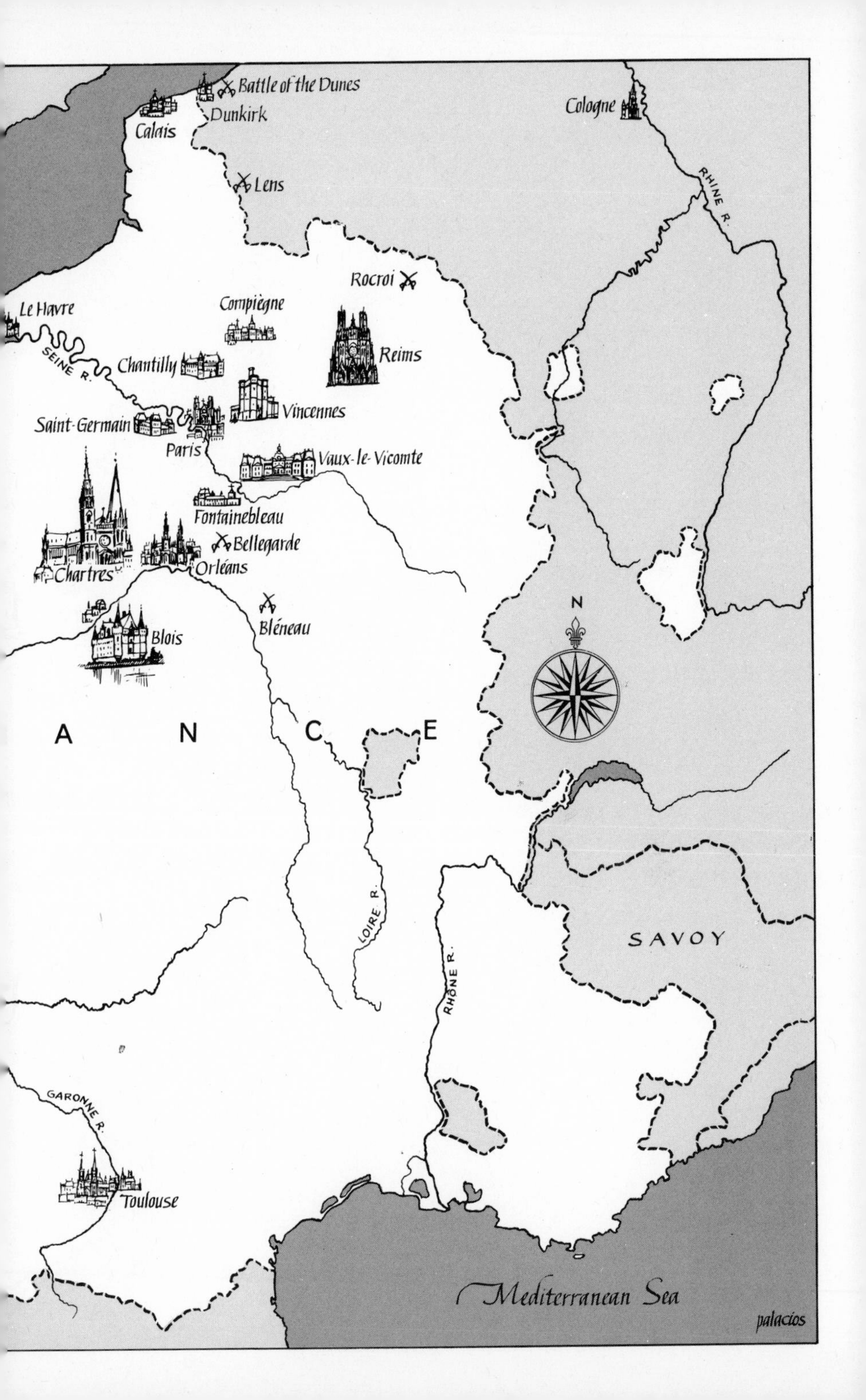
Battle of the Dunes
Dunkirk
Calais
Cologne
Lens
RHINE R.
Rocroi
Le Havre
Compiègne
SEINE R.
Chantilly
Reims
Saint-Germain
Paris
Vincennes
Vaux-le-Vicomte
Fontainebleau
Bellegarde
Chartres
Orléans
N
Bléneau
Blois
A N C E
LOIRE R.
RHÔNE R.
SAVOY
GARONNE R.
Toulouse
Mediterranean Sea
palacios

PART I

THE EARLY YEARS

I. A DAUPHIN FOR FRANCE

It was nearly noon. Under the high, slow-moving clouds of France, the royal castle of Saint-Germain seemed from afar to be drowsing. But inside the somber pile—behind the wide medieval moat and slender Renaissance turrets—there was great activity.

Cannoneers on the ramparts manned their guns. Fifty mounted couriers waited on horseback in the courtyard to carry the news to the far corners of France. In the long galleries musketeers in blue and silver cloaks stood guard by the score.

It was September 5, 1638, in the twenty-eighth year of the reign of King Louis XIII. And the long-awaited news was this: after many years of mixed hope and disappointment, Anne of Austria, Queen of France, was giving birth to her first child.

A small crowd had gathered in the state bedroom. King Louis was there, restless and self-centered even in this hour of his wife's ordeal. His brother, Gaston, for many years heir to the throne, craned his handsome head and long neck over the people around the bed, as if to make sure that there was no trickery afoot. Others sharing the great moment were the Princes of the Blood and the Constable de Montmorency. The Duchesse de Vandôme, the Comtesse de Soissons, and the Marquise de Lansac, governess-to-be, were also in attendance.

The witnesses were present by the law of the land, for from birth to death royalty had no privacy.

The labor proved long and difficult. At one point it looked as if the Queen's life was in danger.

"Save the child!" said Louis to one of the weeping ladies. "There will be plenty of chance to mourn the mother."

At last, just before high noon of that fifth day of September, the baby was born, and the mother was seen to be out of danger.

"It's a dauphin!" the triumphant cry went up.

This was the time-honored title of the heir to the throne of France. *Dauphin* is the French word for dolphin. For reasons lost in history, the lord of Vienne, an ancient city on the Rhône, was known in the Middle Ages as the "Dauphin de Vienne." When Vienne and its province of Dauphiné became part of France in 1349, the king agreed that his eldest son should take the title of Dauphin de Vienne, in much the same way that the English heir apparent became Prince of Wales.

The cannons boomed the news from the ramparts, and the church bells of the town of Saint-Germain took up the cry. Across the clanging drawbridge the messengers spurred north and south, east and west.

The good people of Saint-Germain were ready for the event. The tank that fed the fountain in the square had been filled with red wine. Now, from four silver dolphins the streams of dark liquid gushed out. The townsfolk drank and drank again in honor of the newborn prince.

Nearby Paris was ready, too. When the news reached the city, forty pieces of artillery roared in sequence and three hundred bombs flared and burst. For the next forty-eight hours the capital gave itself up to dances, fireworks, open-air banquets, concerts, parades, triumphal floats.

All France joined in. It was a kind of national delirium. The nation was in the mood for joy. Vigorous, powerful, already the most populous country in Europe, she was emerging from a long period of strife. Now there was a son of France. Now the fair land could have a focus and a future. . . .

At the urging of others in the royal bedchamber, the King approached the bedside and embraced his wife. Then he hurried off to the high Gothic chapel of the castle (where he felt much more at home) to give thanks to heaven for the son who had been born.

Meanwhile, Madame de Lansac, the new royal governess, was fulfilling her first duties. She wrapped the child in a blue blanket embroidered with the golden lilies of France. Then she carried the precious bundle to quarters that had been prepared in another part of the castle. As she walked down the long galleries, the musketeers raised their swords in flashing salute.

It was both fitting and prophetic that Louis, soon to become the Fourteenth of his name, was born near noon of that far-off September. For during his seventy-three year reign, the longest recorded reign in history, France reached the meridian of her greatness. And Louis took the sun as his emblem. It is as the Sun King—perhaps the most dazzling monarch the world has ever seen—that he will always be remembered.

2. A WINTRY KING, A GIDDY QUEEN

The new Dauphin of France turned out to be a healthy child and a cheerful one. His parents called him Louis, after his father and many other kings of France back to the dim beginnings of history. Cardinal Richelieu, the great Prime Minister, suggested he also be called *le Dieudonné*, which is French for The Godgiven. Everyone agreed that this was appropriate.

It was well known that King Louis XIII and his queen, called all her life Anne of Austria, had been on bad terms for years and avoided each other as much as possible. A strange, moody man, Louis liked hunting and making war far better than he liked women and making love. He spent a good deal of time at his hunting lodge at Versailles, where no women were welcome. But one night late in the year 1637 a sudden storm forced him to stay in Paris. He took supper with the Queen at the gloomy old palace called the Louvre, and spent the night there.

Exactly nine months later the Dauphin was born.

The fact that he was such a healthy child was almost as much of a miracle as the birth itself. For he had a legacy of ill health on his father's side, and he came from tired stock on his mother's.

Even though Louis XIII was the son of Henry of Navarre, that vigorous mountain prince who was the first Bourbon king of France, he suffered from a whole variety of ailments. Chronic tuberculosis and chronic melancholy were just two of them. He was beardless until he was over twenty-one, then grew the splendid beard and mustaches which set the fashion of the day. He had black eyes in a white, haggard face, and his normal expression was both vacant and cruel.

As for Anne of Austria, she was a Hapsburg, a sister of King Philip IV of Spain. The many portraits of Philip by Velázquez tell us a lot: in the pale eyes, slack mouth, and petulantly jutting chin we can read the degeneracy of a whole race of emperors and kings.

Anne herself was plump and pleasant to look at, with beautiful hands, chestnut hair, and wonderful green eyes. Frivolous and vain, she loved gossip, dancing, and the intrigues of the Court. She could hardly wait for her ailing husband to die so that she could be Regent of France.

All the rest of her life she would adore her first-born son, although she would neglect him shamefully from time to time. Louis XIII, on the other hand, after a few short months of paternal pride, became jealous of the health and promise of his son.

One day, King Louis and his favorite companion, the young Marquis de Cinq-Mars, were visiting the two-year-old Dauphin. Cinq-Mars tried to fondle the child, who started to scream. Louis XIII intervened. Louis the God-given screamed louder still.

"What a strange upbringing!" the King said furiously. "My own son can't stand the sight of me. We'll soon put this right."

He wrote promptly to Cardinal Richelieu in the same vein:

"I am very dissatisfied with my son. As soon as he sees me, he yells as if I were the devil, and cries for his mother. To get over these bad-tempered displays, it is going to be necessary to take him away from his mother as soon as possible."

The Queen learned about this threat quickly enough, for nothing that ever happened at the French Court was secret for long. She and Madame de Lansac took action at once. For several days they hammered away at little Louis. By alternate promises and threats the word was somehow communicated: *he must be nice to his father.*

Five days after his letter of complaint to Cardinal Richelieu, the King wrote quite differently to his minister: "My son played with me for a full hour . . . we are the best friends in the world."

And again, a day later: "My son can't get along without me; he wants to follow me everywhere."

So, at two, Louis the Dauphin had already learned to mask his true feelings.

Not long after this episode, a second son was born to Louis and Anne. He was called Philip and given the traditional title of Duc d'Anjou. Now the succession, so long in doubt, was doubly safe.

For some reason, Louis XIII welcomed his second son with more warmth than he had the first. He even smiled one of his wintry smiles.

When the Dauphin was four, he was christened at a state ceremony. Afterward, still in his robe of silver cloth, the child came to see his father, bedridden now and with not much time left to live.

"What are you called at present?" Louis asked his son.

"Louis XIV, Papa."

"Not yet, my son, not yet!"

3. TIME OF CHANGE

Back in 1624, when Louis XIII made Cardinal Richelieu his First Minister, the country had been riddled with problems both at home and abroad. The Protestants–Huguenots as they were called–were so powerful they were almost a state-within-a-state. The great nobles, traditionally almost peers or equals of the king, plotted endlessly to destroy both monarch and minister. Hapsburg power held French territory in a vise from north and south. With no navy, France was also vulnerable to Atlantic attack from the west.

The King and his minister seemed an extremely ill matched pair. Louis' tastes were simple. He liked to shoe horses, forge locks, train little hunting birds. He enjoyed the company of huntsmen and foot soldiers and was quite ill at ease at his own Court. Shaving people gave him pleasure, and he even liked to make his own bed.

Richelieu was far more royal than the King. His high, noble features were more impressive–the pointed mustaches and elegant spiked beard seemed to have an arrogant life of their own. His tastes were imperial too. Perhaps because he came from country nobility (from a remote part of

France below the Loire called Poitou) he loved the manifestations of power—palaces, sculpture, paintings, formal gardens with fountains and waterfalls. He was as brilliant as his master was slow and suspicious.

What bound and held them was their love of France. Louis had a firm sense of kingly duty. And Richelieu knew very well that a strong central authority, built around the *mystique* of monarchy, was the surest way to expand the nation's power and his own.

By 1642, when King Louis and Richelieu were both dying men, their long coalition was beginning to bring rich rewards. The Huguenots were humbled, the nobles mostly subdued. A standing army and a fleet in being were winning victories over the Hapsburg might.

Although there were days when he still hunted and trained his little birds, the King was slowly sinking. At fifty-seven, Richelieu too was an exhausted man, his body racked by fever, ravaged by ulcer and abscess. He worked mostly from his bed, keeping three secretaries busy and the tapers burning until late at night. There was still so much to be done!

During Richelieu's last days Louis XIII came and sat beside his bed and even fed him consommé with his own hand. Richelieu died in December of 1642, and the King's grief was genuine and deep.

It couldn't have been much fun for young Louis that winter. He was only four and Philip, his brother, barely two. The Court was at Saint-Germain most of the time, first in mourning for the Cardinal, then in some semblance of grief over the King's growing weakness.

There was an unkind story at the time that you could

read the state of the King's health in the faces of his courtiers. If their expressions were gloomy, he had taken a turn for the better. If their faces were wreathed in smiles, he was sinking again.

It is actually hard to believe that Louis XIII survived the ministrations of his doctors as long as he did. In the last year of his life he was bled 47 times, fed 212 different drugs, and given 215 enemas. Still, by some miracle, he clung to life. His skin was yellow white now, his cough an agony.

One day a courtier asked the little Dauphin a curved question. "If God takes your good father, would you wish to be king in his place?"

"No," said Louis, bursting into tears. "I don't want to be king! If Papa dies, I shall throw myself into the moat of the château."

Anne of Austria, too, seems to have had a change of heart. She sat by the King's bed for hours. Often she wept uncontrollably, and had to be led away.

The King was not wholly convinced by these demonstrations of grief.

Once he heard sounds of laughter from the next room.

"That must be the Queen and my brother," he complained.

His confessor, Father Dinet, urged him to think better of the Queen than that.

"In the condition I'm in," said Louis, "I am obliged to forgive her; I am not obliged to believe her."

He often thought about what would happen to his kingdom after he was gone. Remembering his own foolish mother, Marie de' Medici, whose regency had been disastrous, he was anxious to trim the power that would come to Anne as regent. So he decreed in his will that a Council of seven be created, at which the Queen would preside. But each member would have an equal vote.

By May of 1643 it was clear that the end was near. As the hours dragged past, Louis lay in a deep sleep that was like a coma. On the morning of May 10, the Prince de Condé was taking his turn at the bedside. It seemed unlikely that the King would ever regain consciousness.

Suddenly Louis raised himself on his elbow, his eyes alight.

"I dreamt that your son, the Duc d'Enghien, had come to grips with our enemies and that the battle was very stubborn and violent. . . . For a long time the outcome hung in the balance. But victory was ours at last, and we remained masters of the field."

His dream, his moment of vision, would soon come true. Nine days later—five days after Louis' death—the young duke won the great, bitterly fought battle of Rocroi.

The death itself was tranquil. When the doctors warned Louis that the time was near, he took a last farewell of the Queen, the Dauphin, and the little Duc d'Anjou.

The bedchamber was crowded and it was stiflingly hot. The Princes of the Blood were there, the twelve great dukes and peers of France, and the high officials of the realm.

Despite the heat, the King ordered no one to leave, for he knew well that there was no such thing as privacy for a king of France—even to die in. He did signal for more air, and another window was quickly opened onto the bright May afternoon.

From around his neck Louis took a small crucifix and gave it to Father Dinet. At the same time he whispered to the confessor that the cross was for Sister Louise-Angélique, whom he had loved in his strange way when she was Mademoiselle de Lafayette.

His breathing began to grow short.

"Jesus!" he gasped.

He signaled to the confessor, urging him again to keep his errand secret. Then he managed one of his rare smiles. He died with one finger on his lips in the gesture of silence.

Thus the Dauphin became king, and the sun of Louis XIV began to go up the sky.

4. THE MIGHTY VICTORY

How much did Louis remember later of his father's death and the great battle which followed it so closely? How much does any boy of four remember in afterlife? Odds and ends at most–scraps of memory that surface like flotsam spinning upward from a drowned ship.

Three-quarters of a century later, when he was near death, Louis XIV said, "I have loved war too much." There is no doubt that this passion started when he was very young. He had a whole army of toy soldiers, made for him by a silversmith of Nancy–pikemen, musketeers, cavalry-men, gunners–perfect in every detail. Even the miniature silver cannon were cast in the six calibers then in use.

Pistols and muskets and the beautiful cup-hilted swords of the time fascinated him, and he learned their use early, first with scaled-down models, then with the real thing.

In the gardens of the Palais Royal, where the Queen Regent and her two sons lived when they were in Paris, a children's fort was built–small-scale but quite perfect. Young Louis and Philip and their friends took turns storm-ing and defending it.

Without a doubt, the news of the great victory of Rocroi,

coming so soon after his father's death, made a profound impression on Louis, already a warrior-in-the-making.

In Germany and Italy, in the Low Countries and along the Spanish border, there was still some fighting. But in its third decade, the Thirty Years' War, as it is known to history, had reached a weary stalemate.

Like the double eagle on its famous crest, the Hapsburg power had two heads and one strong dynastic heart. The two heads were Philip IV of Spain and his cousin the Holy Roman Emperor, Ferdinand III.

The combined population of the Hapsburg lands was greater than that of the French. Spain was a kingdom of five million people. The Holy Roman Empire–including Germany, Austria, Bohemia, and Hungary–had over twenty million. But Spanish leadership was weary, and the empire was more legacy and legend than political reality. By contrast, France, with some nineteen million inhabitants, was already the biggest single nation in Europe, and she was young, bursting with vigor and ambition.

In the spring of 1643 a new spirit seemed to animate the still-formidable Hapsburg forces. Philip IV's cautious Prime Minister, Olivares, retired. Younger, more aggressive men became the King's advisers. Don Francisco de Melo, who governed the Low Countries for the King of Spain, was one of these. He invaded France from the north and laid siege to the fortified town of Rocroi in the forest country of the Ardennes.

Not long before, the dying Louis XIII had appointed his cousin, the Duc d'Enghien, eldest son of the Prince de Condé, as commander of the French forces in the north.

At twenty-two, the Duke, later known as the Great

Condé, was already a brilliant leader of men. He had a quick, intuitive way of spotting enemy weakness during battle, and he loved the shock of a cavalry charge and the clash of naked steel on steel. With his beaked nose and hooded eyes, he had the look of a young eagle, and his flashing temper matched his sword.

With commendable caution Louis XIII appointed a seasoned old soldier called the Marshal de l'Hôpital as second in command to his bold young kinsman.

De Melo's forces outnumbered young Condé's by four thousand men; he had fifteen thousand infantrymen and eight thousand cavalry, while the French foot soldiers totaled twelve thousand and the cavalry seven thousand. The Spanish soldiers, who fought in big, beautifully disciplined squares, were still the most feared in the world.

Marshal de l'Hôpital was against giving battle even though the French garrison of Rocroi was very close to surrender.

But the young Duke was aflame for action. "I mean to fight, and will answer for the issue," he said.

Condé knew something that no one else knew, and it spurred him on. A private messenger had brought him news of the King's death. Now, more than ever, he wanted to win the wreath of victory for his late cousin and master. Louis XIII may have been a strange, moody man but he was a fighting king!

The road to Rocroi was a narrow defile through scrub forests of spruce and fir. Condé pushed his troops down this bottleneck, wedging it like a cork, so tightly that there was no choice for either side but to fight.

It was six in the evening when the French troops fanned

out, taking up their position within cannon shot of the enemy. The day was fine and there was still plenty of light to attack by. Suddenly one of Condé's officers, a cavalryman named Senneterre, unleashed a charge against the Spanish right. Since his horsemen were on low ground, the charge–which was meant to circle the Spanish lines and relieve the town of Rocroi–involved a fully-exposed gallop across the well-placed Spanish infantry. Not only would it have been very costly indeed, it was a flagrant act of disobedience.

Condé moved like lightning. Spurring to intercept his horsemen, he ordered Senneterre to call off the charge. Reinforcements from his own right wing covered the withdrawal, and night fell before any further, more coordinated action could be started.

While the men were making camp for the night, Condé passed from regiment to regiment. Here he exchanged a word or two, there a joke and a laugh.

Finally, he wrapped himself in his military cloak and went to sleep by the campfire of his Picardy regiment. He slept so soundly that his officers had trouble waking him in the hour before dawn.

Condé himself commanded the French right flank. Between his forces and De Melo's lay a narrow strip of woodland which half-screened the enemy left. Here the Spaniard had placed some sharpshooting musketeers to slow the French attack when it came.

At daybreak Condé moved swiftly forward. The onslaught was so sudden that the musketeers were overwhelmed before the cavalry of the Spanish left wing, which they were protecting, quite realized what had happened.

After a short but furious hand-to-hand fight, the Spanish

horsemen broke and fled the field. Condé swung sharply to the left, toward the Spanish center. Sensing where weakness lay, he charged between the first and second lines. The first line held fast, but the second and third—Italian, German, and Flemish troops—wavered, then gave way.

The magnificent Spanish infantry, some eight thousand strong, was now all but surrounded; nevertheless it still held firm. They were commanded by the heroic Count of Fuentès, who was eighty years old and so gout-ridden that two men had to carry him onto the field in a litter.

Condé led three charges of mixed cavalry and infantry. All three splintered against the musket fire and the long pikes of the solid infantry squares.

Now the Spanish cavalry came streaming out of the forest in a last desperate charge. They were beaten off, and Condé, naked sword in hand, attacked again.

This time the Spanish infantry broke and scattered. One of their officers waved a white flag in surrender, and Condé, with a few of his officers, moved toward the high ground to receive it.

Just at this moment some of the enemy soldiers, thinking that Condé was still attacking, fired a ragged volley. The duke was unhurt, but his men went wild with anger. They butchered hundreds of Spaniards, many of whom had already laid down their arms.

Some Spaniards clung to Condé's stirrups, claiming sanctuary. But they were a pathetic handful in the midst of the general slaughter.

Pleading, cursing, laying about him with the flat of his sword, Condé was at last able to calm his men.

Still on horseback, he surveyed the field. Among all the twisted bodies and broken gun carriages, he saw the life-

less form of the Count of Fuentès. He was lying in his overturned litter, his white beard stained with blood.

Condé took off his plumed hat in salute to the fallen foe.

"If I had not won," he said, "I would wish to have died as honorably as he who lies here."

One of his officers rode up waving the baton of Don Francisco de Melo. The Spanish commander had thrown it away in his haste to escape the stricken field.

Now the victorious French leader questioned one of the Spanish prisoners concerning the number of their forces that had taken part.

"Count the dead," was the proud reply.

It was almost true. The Spanish had lost over fifteen thousand men–killed, wounded, and prisoners–as well as 170 battle flags and 24 cannon.

So the myth of the Spanish phalanx was broken forever, and the legend of a bold new captain was born. Rocroi ended Spanish supremacy by land, just as the defeat of the Armada by the English had broken Spain's sea power nearly sixty years before.

No seamark in the English Channel commemorates the watery grave of the Armada galleons. But there is a little gray obelisk in the fields outside Rocroi on the exact spot where the Spanish infantry, and the legend of its invincibility, died so hard.

When the news reached Paris three hundred miles to the south, there were victory cannonades and grateful Te Deums in the churches. It was a fine omen for the new reign.

As for young Louis–not yet five–his main thought amid all the general joy is not hard to guess: *Please let there still be glory left for me when I am grown.*

5. THE RISE OF GIULIO MAZARINI

Anne of Austria, Queen of France, had two loves. The first, as every reader of Alexandre Dumas' *The Three Musketeers* knows well, was the dashing Duke of Buckingham. He died under an assassin's knife in 1627 while fitting out an English fleet to invade France. He wanted to help free the Protestant city of La Rochelle, and he wanted to see the Queen again.

Her second love was Giulio Mazarini, the subtle Italian adventurer known to history as Jules Mazarin.

Even for the gaudy seventeenth century his career was spectacular. He was a layman who never took priestly orders, yet he reached the rank of Cardinal in the Church. He never became a French subject, yet he rose to be Prime Minister of France.

Cardinal Richelieu presented Mazarin to the Queen as early as 1631. The Italian was then an ambassador, or nuncio, of the Pope, but he was already under the spell—and perhaps in the pay—of the French statesman.

"You will like him very well," said Richelieu insolently to Anne of Austria. "He has the look of Buckingham about him."

This was true. The Englishman and the Italian were men

who rose in life by looks and charm. Both were handsome, with a certain resemblance—more trick than real—of strong features, agreeable eyes, and fine, full mustaches.

One of Mazarin's grandfathers had been a Sicilian fisherman. His father was a minor official in the palace of the great Colonna family in Rome. The famous Barberini Pope, Urban VIII, took a liking to Giulio and became his patron and protector. For a time Mazarin served as a captain in the Pope's private army.

It was in this period that Mazarin first caught the eye of Richelieu. The time was October 1630. Spanish forces under Marshal de Schomberg were closing in on the French-held city of Casale in northern Italy. The strong French troops drawn up under the walls of the city were a few hundred yards from the foe, and about to attack.

Suddenly a lone rider galloped onto the scene, waving a flag of truce.

"Peace! Peace!" he cried.

Some bullets fell about him but the French hesitated long enough to learn his message.

It was Mazarin. He had persuaded the Spanish to raise the siege provided the French turned the fortress of Casale back to the Duke of Mantua.

Richelieu, who was very warlike, was not entirely pleased. When he and Mazarin met for the first time shortly afterward, he was haughty and distant.

As for Mazarin, he was dazzled by the great, wintry Prime Minister.

"I resolved to devote myself to him entirely," he wrote.

Besides, an astrologer had predicted that his own fate lay in France, and that a Cardinal's hat would be his reward before he was forty.

Nominally, he remained the Pope's man. But by 1638 he was so keen to work openly for his French master that he wrote a friend in Rome that he was willing to do so "even if it is a matter of putting up statues or minding the castle."

By 1640 his dream came true and he joined Richelieu's staff. The French minister now saw at first-hand the tact and diplomatic skill of his disciple. In December of 1641, Mazarin received the Cardinal's hat with the somewhat grudging approval of his former patron, Pope Urban. Mazarin was thirty-nine.

When Richelieu lay dying, he recommended Mazarin, among several others, to the King. "Your Majesty has Cardinal Mazarin," he said. "I believe no one is more capable of serving his king."

When young Louis was christened, Mazarin was one of the two godparents—privilege indeed. The other was the Princesse de Condé, mother of the great soldier.

During the anxious months between Richelieu's death and the King's, Mazarin was especially useful to Queen Anne. Although she had known him for twelve years, she was now aware as never before of his worldly charm and the pleasures of his company.

Four days after Louis XIII's death she announced, as Queen Regent, that Jules Mazarin would be the Prime Minister of France. Poor Louis XIII! Even his wish to reduce the Queen's power by appointing a ruling council was ignored. Instead, there was a new Prime Minister, and he was the Queen's own chosen man.

No one knows to this day if Mazarin ever married Anne of Austria. We do know that the Queen was in love with Mazarin, and that he made himself agreeable to her in many ways.

Anne of Austria was very pious. She wore mourning for Louis XIII to her dying day. So her own testimony on the matter of Mazarin may be slightly slanted, interesting as it is:

"I admit I love him," she told a close friend, "tenderly, let me say: but the affection I bear him does not go as far as love, or if it does so without my knowing it, my own senses are not involved; my mind is simply charmed by the beauty of his."

A cynical comment made years later by the Princess Palatine, another intimate of the Queen's, may also be biased:

"The widow of Louis XIII did a much worse thing than love Cardinal Mazarin," said the Princess; "she married him."

Perhaps Mazarin's real love was power. As the Queen's chosen minister, he would now wield it for eighteen stormy years.

When Louis XIV and his brother Philip were very young, the Queen loved them fiercely and protectively, like a she-bear with her cubs. She spent far more time with her two sons than most queenly mothers ever did, pushing the royal baby carriage herself and joining in their games. She much preferred the sturdy young Louis to the dark, delicate little Philip, but did not let this show too much.

With the death of Louis XIII and the rise of Jules Mazarin, all this changed. From the age of five to ten Louis was a neglected and miserable child.

At forty-two Anne of Austria was still a striking woman. She made an impression of rather sleepy good nature, but this concealed a fiery temper. Young Louis, Philip, and

Mazarin all learned to take cover when her usually pleasant voice rose to a sharp and piercing soprano.

We owe a good part of our knowledge of what she was like to one of her ladies-in-waiting, the observant Madame de Motteville. She saw everything, and wrote it all down. Queen Anne, for example, told Madame de Motteville that she loved Buckingham, "but he was never my lover." Certainly, the Englishman had been hustled out of France when his infatuation for the Queen began to show.

Now the situation was quite different. For the first time in her life the widowed Queen had the full attention of a brilliant and fascinating man of the world. They spent long hours conferring together on matters of state. Mazarin spared her much of the tedious business of governing and helped her make the key decisions. Except when her temper took over, she was yielding and obedient.

So there was little time for the Dauphin. Except on state occasions, when he was dressed in plumes and ribbons and carried on a cushion by a Peer of the Realm (as a symbol of his minority), young Louis was left to his governesses and valets and chambermaids.

They, too, were busy with palace life. One day when Louis and Philip were playing soldier in the Palais Royal gardens, Louis fell into a big garden pool. His brother started to howl and at last servants came running. The King was fished out of the water, blue with cold and half-drowned.

For all his elegance, Mazarin was a miser at heart. When he was not on public display, the little King wore frayed doublets and stockings with holes in them. At night he slept in torn sheets that his feet poked through. His one bathrobe had seen such long service that it came well above the royal knees.

Madame de Motteville noted that Louis, who had been so cheerful as a baby, never smiled at his play. Small wonder! The fact was that he was already learning to conceal his feelings—to watch and learn and never show his hand.

Many thought him stupid and dull compared to his light-hearted brother, but this may have been in part because Louis' sense of royal dignity was already so great.

At seven he was taken away from his governesses. The bluff, honest Marshal de Villeroy was appointed tutor, and a man called La Porte became his principal lackey, or valet.

At about this time, Louis' love of wrestling was almost as great as his passion for playing soldier. Sometimes it was hard to tell where boy left off and boy-king began.

One day he and a young cousin, the Comte d'Artois, wrestled each other for so long that La Porte told them enough was enough.

Louis ignored him and continued to roll on the floor with D'Artois.

La Porte sat down, clapping his hat on his head as he did so. Louis noticed at once.

"How can you cover your head in my presence?" he called. "How can you sit without my permission?"

"Pardon, sire," said La Porte, rising and taking off his hat. "I did not think a king was in the room."

Louis released D'Artois at once.

"Monsieur my cousin," he said, "you are at liberty to go."

6. A SOLEMN CHILDHOOD

La Porte was quite a remarkable man. For secret services to Anne of Austria, he had once been imprisoned by Cardinal Richelieu in the Bastille, and threatened with torture in that grim old fortress. The Cardinal wanted to prove that the Queen was in direct communication with her brother, the King of Spain. Since France and Spain were at war, this would have been high treason. La Porte was reported to be acting as private messenger.

La Porte revealed nothing. When he was finally released, the Queen gave him the warmest of welcomes and his first Court appointment.

"Here," said Anne, "is the poor lad who has suffered so much in my behalf, and to whom I owe all that I am today."

The new valet was a seigneur, or gentleman, or he would never have become a member of the immediate staff of the King. Far more to the point, he was a brave and kindly man. He was also, like almost everyone else at Court, a writer of memoirs.

"I was the first man to sleep in the room of His Majesty,"

he noted, "which was something that astonished him at first, not seeing any women close to him any more."

Louis adjusted quickly, and grew very fond of La Porte. At bedtime the valet would read him stories from early French history—stories of strong kings who were their own masters and of weak ones, too, who let themselves be ruled by their chieftains.

This was not quite as innocent a diversion as it seemed. Like so many of the Court, La Porte hated Mazarin as a foreigner and an upstart. So he did his best to turn young Louis against him.

Among La Porte's favorite stories were those about the Merovingian kings of the eighth century, kings so feeble that when traveling, they lay in great wagons rather than ride on horseback.

He planted the thought that Louis just might grow up supine and lazy like these sluggish kings (*rois fainéants*).

Louis was furious.

"I'll never be like that!" he screamed in a rare outburst.

There was actually little danger that he would be. By the age of nine he was a first-class horseman and a crack shot. He fenced very well and he danced, according to Madame de Motteville (who was perhaps easily dazzled) like a young god. Watching him at a Court ball, she described his black satin coat embroidered with gold and silver, and observed that "his fine features, the gentleness and gravity of his eyes, the whiteness and vivacity of his skin, along with his hair, which was very blond at the time, set him off even better than his coat."

Both Louis and La Porte liked to make fun of Mazarin's love of display.

"There goes the Grand Turk," said the little King as they watched the Prime Minister and a large escort sweep past on the terrace of one of the royal castles.

Aware of the boy's growing dislike, Mazarin kept Louis under close watch. He appointed his own minions to be the royal instructors in Spanish and German and Italian, and placed other spies in the household.

Sensing this, Louis became more ingrown than ever. When his first cousin, the Prince of Wales, who would one day rule England as King Charles II, came to visit, they played together in complete silence. Each was overwhelmed by the solemnity of the occasion.

In November of his ninth year, young Louis nearly died. Suddenly, while watching a play at the private theater in the Palais Royal, he complained to the Queen Mother that he felt ill. He was promptly put to bed with what appeared to be a case of smallpox. For a while the disease took its normal course. There was concern, of course, but the "pox" was very common in those days, and it was expected that the King's robust constitution would see him through.

Then, on the eleventh day, his temperature shot way up and he had a fainting spell.

On the fourteenth day, he lay near death, with his mother sobbing at the foot of the bed and his Uncle Gaston hovering nearby. Gaston tried hard to look as sad as possible, but did not quite succeed. For if Louis died, frail little Philip could be quickly brushed aside or disposed of, and he, the one-time heir, would inherit the kingdom at last.

That night some of Gaston's followers held a merry dinner in his honor, and there were toasts drunk to King

Gaston the First. Mazarin, meanwhile, began to make himself pleasant to these same followers, just in case.

It looked as if France was heading straight for a time of terrible turmoil.

But fate had other plans. Toward midnight, Louis' fever started to fall again. By morning the smallpox was back on its normal course, and soon he was well.

Young Louis had proved a model patient, Madame de Motteville dutifully reported. "He said witty and kind things to all who served him and was docile in doing all the doctors asked him to do."

The severe attack cost him his beauty. The golden boy, the white-skinned child so much admired by all, came out of it with cheeks covered with fiery spots. He would bear some of the scars for life.

7. REGENCY HONEYMOON

Historically, a child-king has always been something of a mixed blessing for any kingdom. Everyone tries to grab a little more power for himself. The Court is riddled with intrigue. The game of "favorites"—always prevalent in any palace—goes on more furiously than ever.

The minority of Louis XIV was typical. The great nobles, so long and so ruthlessly kept in their place by Cardinal Richelieu, began to stir and dream again. The Princes of the Blood—those cousins of the King just outside his immediate family—grew restless. Uncle Gaston, the feckless Duke of Orleans, resumed his endless plotting. He had been vividly reminded by his nephew's near-fatal smallpox attack that the King was quite capable of dying. With a little good luck and bad health, the glittering heritage could still be his!

Although well under forty, Gaston was a man old in conspiracy if not in wisdom. Every featherbrained scheme to topple Louis XIII and Richelieu during the years of their great coalition had had his support. Invariably the plots were discovered, Gaston confessed his complicity, and the ringleaders were beheaded. As the King's brother, Gaston had a certain immunity. But Louis XIII, toward the end of his life, kept the shiftless Gaston in more or less permanent exile in the fine old castle of Blois on the Loire.

Gaston was big, handsome, and healthy. He had his share of the Bourbon charm, and a cheerful habit of whistling his way down the gloomy galleries of the Louvre. Once, in a state meeting, he whistled and hummed for half an hour at a stretch.

Cardinal de Retz, whose memoirs are among the most vivid of the time, described Gaston in a devastating sentence: "The Duc d'Orleans possessed all the good qualities requisite for a man of honor except the quality of courage."

By his first wife, Gaston had a daughter, Anne, the Duchesse de Montpensier, known to history as the Great Mademoiselle. She was as brave and bold as her father was cowardly.

Ultimately, the most troublesome of all the restless elements stirring in France was the Parlement of Paris. Long ignored and often suppressed, the Parlement existed mainly to put its seal of approval on royal edicts and decrees. Composed mostly of lawyers and other professional men, it also acted as the highest judicial body in the land. Its members were appointed by the King, not elected—with membership often passing from father to son or uncle to nephew.

Now, in the mid-1640s, the Parlement began to see itself in a larger political role. Its members were excited by what was happening across the Channel in England. There Oliver Cromwell and the British Parliament were in full revolt against King Charles I. Civil war was raging, soon to be climaxed by the trial and execution of the King.

Events in France itself also gave the members of Parlement ideas.

Shortly after his father's death, young Louis had appeared before the Paris Parlement in a ceremony called a *lit de justice.* In this ritual, dating from the Middle Ages, the King presided from a raised dais. On the steps below him, in descending order, sat his family, the Princes of the Blood, the great nobles, and the Royal Council, with the members of the Parlement filling the rest of the hall. The purpose of a *lit de justice*, usually summoned in time of emergency, was to inform the Parlement of the royal wishes.

At this first appearance, young Louis, who was not yet five, had little to say. But he said it very well and from memory:

"Messieurs, I have come to testify my affection and good will toward my Parlement. My Chancellor will tell you the rest."

Louis glanced at his mother, and Anne of Austria smiled her approval.

In her plump, pleasant voice the Queen Mother told the Parlement that she "would be happy to have their counsel on all occasions." Gaston d'Orleans, on his best behavior for once, protested his love and loyalty for the Queen, and the Great Condé did the same.

Then the Chancellor, an old man called Séguier, impressive in his violet robes trimmed with ermine, informed the Parlement that the King wished to name his mother Regent of France, "for the free, absolute, and entire administration of the affairs of the kingdom during his minority."

It was the first time in years that the ambitious and able members of the Parlement had even been asked to approve anything. The fact that the King's request was not quite what his late father had in mind was really an added argument in favor, for Louis XIII had been a hard and heavy-handed master. Approval of the Queen Mother as Regent was quickly and unanimously voted.

So a vista opened up, promising the Parlement a real share in the affairs of state. Soon after, when the new Regent announced that Cardinal Mazarin was her choice for Prime Minister, the Parlement dutifully endorsed it.

At first all went wonderfully well. The Queen and her beloved minister began their joint rule in a gentle and generous mood. The princes and other great nobles were given new honors and lands which they had scarcely deserved. The Parlement was flattered and consulted as it had not been in years. Commenting on the royal generosity, Cardinal de Retz made a cynical entry in those famous memoirs: "The French language contains but five words: 'The Queen is so good.' "

Young Louis, more and more neglected now, went back to his torn sheets, his toy cannon, and his dreams of glory.

8. FRANCE ON TWO BRINKS

By the middle 1640s the relationship between Court and Parlement was beginning to sour. While the members continued to protest their love and loyalty to the boy King, they made it clearer and clearer that they disliked Cardinal Mazarin very much indeed.

The worst disagreement was over money.

Like the other, greater Cardinal before him, Mazarin had mixed views on the subject. Richelieu and he both recognized that money was vital to power—in paying for the standing army which maintained such power and in providing the pomp and splendor which were its visible proof. But they simply instructed the Parlement on what was needed and expected to have their edicts for more taxation quickly approved.

Now the peasants of France, on whom the heaviest burden always seemed to fall, could only be squeezed so much. By 1645 they were almost ruined. What was new was that the Parlement, for almost the first time in French history, was beginning to show some sympathy for their hard lot.

At a second *lit de justice*, much less friendly than the first, Omer Talon, the vigorous and outspoken Attorney General, was extremely critical. He described the people of France as ruined by the needless wars. He even went down on his knees before the Queen Regent and begged her to have pity on their suffering.

Meanwhile Mazarin, busy with war and foreign policy, failed to realize the mood of the Parlement and the people.

"Let the French get used to my way of acting if they will," he remarked, "because I have no wish to get used to theirs. When King and Queen Mother are for me, all Frenchmen are my friends–and if I were to fall into disgrace with them, I would have nothing more to do with the French, for I would not stay in France."

This was high-handed folly, as soon become apparent.

By 1648, at a third *lit de justice*, Omer Talon was bolder than ever. This time he spoke directly to young Louis.

"You are, sire, our sovereign lord. Your power comes from heaven and need not account for its action, after God, except to your conscience. But it is of concern to your glory that we be free men and not slaves."

These were strong words at a time when the divine right of kings was only just beginning to be questioned.

While his tone remained respectful, Omer Talon's words grew stronger still.

"For ten years now the countryside is ruined, the peasants reduced to sleeping on straw, their furniture sold to pay the taxes which they can never satisfy."

Then he turned to the Queen Regent, only this time he did not go down on his knees.

"I beg you, Madam, give some kind of thought in the secrecy of your heart to this public misery . . . think, too, of the disastrous state of the provinces, where the hope of peace and the honor of victories cannot nourish those who have no bread and who cannot consider such palms and laurels among the ordinary fruits of earth."

Once back in the Palais Royal the Queen wept and her voice went shrill.

"My son will punish them! My son will punish them!" she screamed, lumping Omer Talon and all the other members of Parlement into one rebellious body.

Still fascinated with each other and their own power, Anne of Austria and Mazarin now realized that they could no longer afford to ignore or neglect the young King. With his manly way of sitting a horse, his dignity and his good looks (for the smallpox scars were a familiar and not too disfiguring mark of the times), he was their best asset. The people of Paris still cheered when they put him on display, which they did more and more often.

An anecdote of the time shows that young Louis, almost ten now, was not unaware of his new status.

While stag-hunting one day, he noticed that one of his courtiers was wearing an unusual doublet of white linen. The King admired the doublet and ordered a copy to be made for himself.

"I want it fast," he said. "I couldn't care less if it costs a hundred pistoles more, as long as I get it within two hours."

He got the doublet on the double.

Meanwhile France's military campaigns were going very well indeed. In those times making war was a more natural condition than being at peace. It suited Cardinal Mazarin to have the hot-blooded nobles off fighting, and it suited the nobles to fight. If they didn't fight the enemies of France, they plotted against the Crown or they brawled among themselves. Even in the decade from 1642–1652, a time of many campaigns, they managed to kill nine hundred of their own number in duels.

The Great Condé's victory at Rocroi was followed by many others. At Fribourg, in 1644, he developed a new technique for engaging the foe at close range. He simply threw his marshal's baton into the enemy trenches. Then, sword in hand, he would go in and recover it like a dog chasing a stick.

Three years later the young eagle did receive one setback when he was laying siege to Lérida in northeast Spain. It was a formal seventeenth-century siege and thus was carried out with a good deal of ritual. The Governor of Lérida, Don Antonio Britte, sent his opponent a glass of lemonade each morning. But during the day Don Antonio sallied out of the city gates in such spirited attacks that French morale grew low and desertions were high. Finally Condé, restless, not really suited to siege warfare, broke off the operation.

Now another great soldier came on stage to match the fame of Condé. His name was Henri de la Tour d'Auvergne, Vicomte de Turenne. He was a younger brother of the Duc de Bouillon, who was one of the most powerful nobles of France and among the least reliable. Turenne himself was the steadiest of men. He was cautious but never timid, and he handled troops with born skill. He provided the perfect balance for Condé's inspired dash and bravado.

His valor and his sound judgment had earned him the proud title of Marshal of France as early as 1643, when he was still in his twenties. In his person he was square and solid where Condé was lean. He had good level eyes, a sensible mustache, and a beard like a little dagger.

Together the Great Condé and the Vicomte de Turenne would write some glorious pages in the history of France, and one or two that are as gaudy and puzzling as the age in which they lived.

By the summer of 1648, the Great Condé was back in fighting form. Slightly outnumbered by the army of the Archduke Leopold, younger brother of the Holy Roman Emperor Ferdinand III, he and some fifteen thousand men were withdrawing in good order across the Belgian border into northern France. Sensing the exact moment, Condé doubled back. On August 2, at Lens—a few miles northeast of Arras—he attacked Leopold on the march, achieving tactical surprise. "Remember Rocroi!" was Condé's battle cry as he led the assault. The surging French inflicted heavy losses, and Leopold's army reeled back into Belgium, with the French in harrying pursuit.

When young Louis heard the news, his comment showed how politically shrewd he had already become.

"The messieurs in Parlement will be quite unhappy about this," he said.

He was right. Mazarin's reputation with the Parlement was so low that its members had been openly urging his dismissal. The victory of Lens boosted his prestige, and stilled his critics for the moment.

Taking stock, the Cardinal realized that it was time to end the long war. With the army home at last, the tax burden of campaigning would be eased. Durable peace must be made so that Parlement could be confined once more to its normal modest role.

Events of the year 1648 moved swiftly. They were quickly to prove how right Mazarin was, and also how wrong. For this was the year that France, poised on the brinks of domestic chaos and of foreign peace as well, plunged over both.

PART II

THE YEARS OF TUMULT

9. THE SLINGSHOT TIME

The four noisy years from 1648 to 1652 are known to history as the Fronde. The word is French for sling, and it was used by Cardinal Mazarin in a scornful reference to the members of the Parlement and their supporters. He compared them to schoolboys in the Paris streets who would fire their slingshots at everything in sight but scatter when the civil guards appeared on the scene. Then, after the patrol had passed, they would start making trouble again.

The comparison stuck. Those who took Parlement's side in its struggles with the Queen Regent and Mazarin became known as *frondeurs*, or slingshot carriers. Accepting the label, they promptly started wearing hatbands made of a loop of cord like a sling.

The years of the Fronde were part of France's growing pains—a last disease of childhood as the nation neared maturity. No one behaved very well, from Queen Regent and Prime Minister down. Dazzling women like Condé's sister, the Duchesse de Longueville, and glory-hunting ones like the Great Mademoiselle, had far more power than they deserved. Born troublemakers like the Cardinal de Retz bobbed naturally to the surface. Even steady, sturdy Turenne lost his common sense for a while.

We don't really know what young Louis' thoughts were during the Fronde, but we do know what he learned, and how in later life he made very sure no such lawless time ever happened again.

Mazarin and the Parlement stalked each other warily throughout the summer of 1648.

Early in July the Parlement voted a new constitution for France. Its twenty-eight articles were very democratic in spirit and included many safeguards to protect the rights and property of individuals. No man could be held prisoner more than twenty-four hours without a hearing. No new tax was to be imposed, no office created, without the approval of the Parlement's members.

At the same time that it voted these drastic changes, the Parlement protested its loyalty and devotion to young Louis. But the new constitution would have limited his powers very much indeed.

The reforms sought by the Parlement were just a little too good to be true. The fact was that its members had a vested interest in the collecting of taxes. The system had been thoroughly corrupt for a long time, and the Parlement was at the heart of the corruption. Nor were the members the true voice of the people, for they were appointed by the Crown, not elected.

They assumed a virtue they did not have. They were mainly seeking an extension of their own power.

Madame de Motteville summed this up in a terse phrase: "They were all infected with the love of the public good, which they reckoned to be their very own."

Mazarin flattered, twisted, turned, fought for time. When

news came of the victory at Lens, he and Anne of Austria felt strong enough to make their countermove.

On August 28 there was a high mass in the Cathedral of Notre Dame to celebrate the victory. They used it as the occasion for a show of royal force, deploying soldiers at key points around Paris.

As she came out of the Cathedral, Anne beckoned to one of her officers, Comminges by name. For a moment or two they were seen to be in earnest conversation.

Comminges' mission was soon known. That same afternoon three of the most distinguished members of Parlement were arrested: one of them, Counselor Broussel, was an old man much loved by the people of Paris.

All that summer the city had been a powder keg. The arrest of Broussel was the spark that blew it wide open.

Suddenly every man, woman, and child seemed to have a musket, pike, or dagger in his hand. Barrels, filled with earth and linked by iron chains, blocked the streets. (The French word for these barrels was *barrrique*, hence barricade.) Paving stones were torn up to strengthen the barricades. Every store window was shuttered against looting.

By the thousands the Paris mob jammed against the iron gates of the Palais Royal.

"Broussel!" they chanted. "Liberty!"

"Death to Mazarin!"

"Long live the King!"

Now that troublemaker for the sheer joy of making trouble, that most quotable of clerics, Paul de Gondi de Retz moved to stage center.

He took over the role of mediator, shuttling from Parle-

ment to court, from merchants to clergy—seeking to be all things to all men. In the words of the historian Philippe Erlanger, "he was the only bishop in France who ever unleashed a civil war without at least invoking religion as a pretext."

At the time he was coadjutor, or deputy, to his uncle, the Archbishop of Paris. But he is known to history as Cardinal de Retz, so we will call him by that later title.

De Retz was an unusual minister of God. He often wore a dagger in place of a breviary and was a notorious woman-chaser and duelist. During the time when he studied for the Church, he had been quite a brilliant scholar. He was short, swarthy, ugly, and ill made. When Richelieu saw him as a young man, he said, "There's a face for the gibbet." But De Retz did have a certain graceless charm, and his *Mémoires* make the days of the Fronde seem like the middle of last week.

Listen to him setting the mood of that restless summer of 1648:

"The Cardinal [Mazarin] played the part of one who thought himself secure, but was much less confident than he appeared. The Queen affected to be good humored and yet was never more ill tempered. . . . I played the innocent but was not so."

At first he underestimated Mazarin. Here is his famous description: "At the foot of the throne, where the fierce and terrible Richelieu used to thunder rather than govern [was this] mild and gentle successor who was perfectly complacent and extremely troubled that his dignity as Cardinal did not permit him to be as humble to all men as he desired."

On the Day of the Barricades, De Retz urged the Queen Regent to release Broussel as a first step to restoring order.

Anne of Austria was furious.

"There is revolt in imagining that there can ever be a revolt!" she screamed. "Release Broussel? I'd sooner strangle him with my own hands."

Mazarin was still playing for time. He calmed the Queen and finally persuaded her to agree to the release of Broussel and the others provided order was restored.

De Retz and a brave officer called the Marshal la Meilleraye went into the streets to face the howling mob.

De Retz in his bishop's robes moved confidently through the dense crowds, "bestowing benedictions left and right." Beside him, La Meilleraye, drawn sword in hand, thundered the news.

"Liberty for Broussel! Liberty for Broussel! Long live the King!"

As De Retz tells it, more people saw La Meilleraye's drawn sword then heard his words. There was a sudden tumult. De Retz was knocked down by a stone, but managed to scramble to his feet. As he did so, one of the mob—a young man he had never seen before—put a musket to his head.

"Ah, wretch, if your father could see you now!" said De Retz. The rioter, thinking the bishop was a family friend, spared his life.

De Retz's own account of what happened next is not exactly self-effacing:

"With an abundance of flattery, caresses, entreaties, and menaces, I prevailed upon them to lay down their weapons; and it was this which saved the day."

The mob, good humored again, marched De Retz and La Meilleraye back to the Palais Royal to make sure that the promise to release the prisoners was made good.

When they were summoned into the presence of the Queen Regent, the bluff La Meilleraye told her that De Retz had saved Paris. He was full of praise for what the swarthy coadjutor had done.

The Queen was not impressed when the Marshal reported that Paris was in a submissive mood.

"Not so submissive as guilty," she answered, her voice edged with anger. "If the people were so raging as I was made to believe, how came they to be so soon subdued?"

La Meilleraye, in turn, grew angry.

"They are only submissive for the moment," he warned her. "If you do not release Broussel by morning one stone will not be left upon another."

That night De Retz and his boon companions celebrated, savoring the power that seemed to be coming his way.

"Tomorrow before midday," he exulted over the food and wine, "I shall be master of Paris."

On that August afternoon ten-year-old Louis and his friends played as usual in the gardens of the Palais Royal. The palace itself was in no real danger from the mob, for the Swiss and French guards stood firm before it.

Louis and his comrades took turns attacking and defending the toy fort. They did so with more fervor than ever, for the uproar outside the walls could hardly be ignored.

The grown world was moving nearer to the garden.

10. FLIGHT BY STARLIGHT

Dismissing De Retz that day, the Queen Regent fired a parting shot:

"Take the trouble to pray a little to the Lord," she said as he bowed out of the room.

Anne's remark rankled, even as De Retz savored the triumph that would soon be his. He stirred up another riot the next day, and the cries for the release of Broussel and the other members of the Parlement grew louder than ever.

With most of their army still on the frontiers, the Queen and Mazarin really had no choice. That afternoon the prisoners were freed.

So, in a sense, De Retz triumphed and Paris was his. The only trouble was that he didn't know what to do with it, for he had no philosophy, no policy—just the love of intrigue and trouble for their own sakes.

As for Anne, for all her seeming submission to the will of the people of Paris and the smooth words of De Retz, she lived only for revenge.

In the fall of 1648, the brutal, bitter Thirty Years' War came to an end. The Treaty of Westphalia, debated and discussed for over five years, was signed at Münster. This was the Prussian city where, on October 24, the delegates of the warring countries reached the final agreement. Seventy cannon boomed three thunderous salvos from the city walls to hail the ending.

The war had been one of the most disastrous in history. In Germany alone, where many of the campaigns had been fought, eight million people lost their lives. For years, the military had lived off the land, until there was nothing much left for the peasantry but devastation and despair.

By the treaty, the German half of the Hapsburg power was splintered into over a hundred small states and principalities, and never did recover its unity.

France added some valuable border territories in the north and east—Alsace, parts of Artois and Luxembourg. As for the Spanish branch of the Hapsburg dynasty, King Philip IV chose to continue the fight against the French in a war that would flare fitfully for eleven years more.

But for the moment, there was peace at last. The veteran French regiments came swinging down from the north with the Great Condé at their head. As the master diplomat and chief architect of peace, Mazarin's stock began to rise. He and Anne agreed that the time was almost at hand to put Parlement and the mob back in their proper place!

But first of all they must take themselves beyond the reach of riots and barricades, and they must take young Louis with them. Then Paris could be surrounded, besieged, starved into submission.

Louis would never forget the night of their escape. It was early in the new year—January 5, 1649—and it was bone cold, with a powdering of remote stars in the sky.

Louis was given no advance warning of what was planned. As he so often did, he spent the evening playing backgammon with his mother in her private apartments. Madame de Motteville, present as usual, noted that the Queen seemed unusually gay.

Another lady-in-waiting joined the group.

"There is a rumor running through Paris that the Queen will slip away tonight," she whispered to Madame de Motteville.

Madame de Motteville shrugged and pointed to the domestic scene of Anne and Louis at the gaming table.

Before retiring, the Queen held her usual small court, where the gossip of the day was reported and picked apart. She and Louis shared a cake with the various ladies-in-waiting. She yawned, kissed her son good night. Young Louis went dutifully off to bed.

At three in the morning Marshal de Villeroy woke Louis. In silence and secrecy, Villeroy helped him dress. Then, along with little Philip (just as sleepy and even more scared than his older brother), the Marshal led Louis to the iron gates of the Palais Royal where two carriages were waiting.

Anne joined them there. So did Gaston d'Orleans, his wife, and his daughter, the Great Mademoiselle. The carriages moved quickly away through the empty streets. Soon they came to one of the gates in the high, old city wall. After a whispered word with the guard, the gates swung open. The carriages rolled through.

Outside, in the avenue called the Cours-la-Reine which in happier times was a great place to ride and drive, to see and be seen, they were joined by Mazarin in another carriage, and a handful of mounted men.

With the horses' breath making faint plumes in the bitter cold and their hooves striking sparks on the stony roads, the secret cavalcade headed for Saint-Germain.

The winter stars began to fade. The fugitives reached the sleeping town and then at last the big, empty castle at its far end.

11. BREASTPLATES AND VIOLINS

The castle really was empty. In the seventeenth century, monarchs took all their household furnishings along when they moved from castle to castle, or sent them on ahead. This time, to keep their escape secret, the Queen Regent could do neither. Three folding camp beds were brought for Anne and her two sons. Everyone else had to sleep on straw strewn over the stone floors.

There were no panes in the windows, no firewood, and almost no servants.

The Great Mademoiselle, who was a big, cheerful girl of twenty-two, has left us the liveliest account of the three-month interval at Saint-Germain:

> I had no change of linen: my nightgown was washed during the day and my underslip at night. I had no one to dress my hair or attend to my clothes—it was very inconvenient. I ate with Monsieur [her father]; the food was very bad. But I was in high spirits nevertheless, and Monsieur admired me for not complaining. I am not one to let such things trouble me; I'm above bagatelles.

One reason that the Great Mademoiselle was so cheerful was that she was near young Louis. Although they were first cousins and she was eleven years older than he (and he was only eleven at the time), she dreamed of becoming his queen. Long before, Anne of Austria had once, half jokingly, referred to her son as the "petit mari" of Gaston's handsome daughter. Everyone laughed, but the idea became fixed in the Great Mademoiselle's bold and ambitious heart. She was the richest heiress in Europe, the niece of Louis XIII, and the granddaughter of Henry of Navarre. Why shouldn't she marry young Louis? Any less exalted destiny held little appeal for her.

No one else was happy at Saint-Germain after the first excitement had worn off. There wasn't enough food or money for the servants and they were mostly let go. Anne of Austria had to pawn some of her jewels to pay the few that stayed.

From Paris came news of great turmoil. The secret flight of the King from his own capital city was taken as an act of war, and blamed mostly on Mazarin. Suddenly everyone was singing little ditties called "Mazarinades," making fun of the Italian. One of the most popular started like this:

A Fronde-like wind
got up one day;
'Gainst Mazarin
it howls, they say.

On January 8, two days after the flight, Parlement issued a decree declaring Mazarin an enemy of King and State. Pamphleteers, urged on by De Retz, picked up where the verse makers left off. The Paris presses churned out a flood of invective, and the theme was always much the same: "Murder him who knows neither joy nor law nor religion! Murder, murder, murder Mazarin!"

The people of Paris still liked Louis XIV and missed him. "*Vive le roi! Mazarin, non!*" was the popular cry.

Hatred of the foreign Prime Minister bound the conspirators together. As usual De Retz, "witty, debauched, bold, restless" (in the words of the historian Guizot), was everywhere.

First of all he tried to persuade the Great Condé to join the troublemakers of the Fronde. But the young eagle, basking in his own fame, was not yet ready to be corrupted against King and country. De Retz, of course, promised him the sun and the stars, and Condé admitted to the churchman that he was tempted.

"But I am Louis de Bourbon, and will not endanger the State," he said in his final answer.

De Retz turned his charms on Condé's sister, the celebrated Duchesse de Longueville. He managed to convince the Duchesse, a silvery blonde with the face of an angel, that there was a place for her and much power in Paris. She soon fled the icy castle of Saint-Germain, to which she had been summoned by the Queen.

The Duchesse's vain and stupid husband, thirty years her senior, soon followed. So did another brother, a wicked little humpback called the Prince de Conti. His sole claim to fame was his Bourbon blood. He was made the nominal head of the Citizen Army being raised to defend Paris. In fact, all he ever did was what his dazzling sister told him to do.

Another convert was the Duc de la Rochefoucauld–

suave, melancholy, bewitched by the Duchesse. Years later, in retreat and out of his continuing melancholy, he would write the brilliant, cynical *Maximes* which have made his name famous forever.

There was something about the Duchesse which made almost every man who met her want to serve any cause that was hers. De Retz speaks of her "languor," and perhaps it was this—and the fact that she "did not like innocent games" —which made so many rise and follow.

Still another bemused camp follower of the languorous Duchesse was the good steady Vicomte de Turenne. For the only time in his life, the great soldier lost his common sense and threw in his lot with the rebels.

Later in January, a new decree of the Parlement sought to take over all the royal monies in various parts of the kingdom for use in the defense of Paris. Most of France stayed loyal, but the Parlements of Aix and Rouen joined the cause of their Paris brethren.

In February the grim news came from England that Charles I had been beheaded. Here was another harsh example for young Louis why kings must be strong or perish—another compelling argument for putting down the rebellion before it grew too strong!

Slowly, steadily, Condé's troops were drawing a noose around Paris. All shipments of grain were now intercepted. There was yet no assault, but any attempt on the part of the citizens to break out from behind the city walls was countered with vigor.

Strangely enough, Paris was very gay. There was dancing every night at the Hotel de Ville. Nobles who had skirmished all day against Condé's troops outside the walls danced until dawn. One saw, says De Retz, "a commingling of blue scarfs, of ladies, of cuirasses (breastplates) and violins in the town hall, and trumpets in the square."

Then the lack of bread began to hurt. Turenne, too, had been disappointing. He had gone to Germany to recruit mercenaries, but Mazarin bought them off with promises of higher pay. Early in February, Condé's troops, with the young eagle as always in the lead, captured an outpost at Charenton, fortified by the Fronde. It was clear that the citizen troops and the light-hearted noblemen were no match for the seasoned campaigners and their fiery captain.

By March it was all over. There was an amnesty, or general forgiveness. For the time being the Parlement was allowed to keep a good deal of power. One by one the nobles wandered back to Saint-Germain. La Rochefoucauld made the kind of comment that would later be burnished into his *Maximes*: "It is the way of our nation to return to their duty with the same airiness with which they depart from it, and to pass in a single instant from rebellion to obedience."

Mazarin of course held his high post. He and the Queen and young Louis took their time returning to the rebel city. Finally, on August 18, they made a state entry. The King received a thundering welcome, and there were even a few scattered cries of *Vive le Cardinal!* Mazarin was not at all pleased: he had paid hard cash for the cries, and got very little return for his money.

Each side welcomed the breathing spell, but everyone knew that the truce was temporary. For the fever of the Fronde was still strong.

Young Louis, nearing twelve now, was learning fast. The

secret flight, the pawned jewels, the straw bedding held no passing charms for him. More and more he was becoming a sober and silent child–secret, observant, with a dignity beyond his years, and a yearning for security and order which would last throughout his life.

12. THE FRONDE OF THE PRINCES

There was no containing the pride of the Great Condé. As the First Prince of the Blood, the victor of Rocroi and Lens, the soldier who had just tamed Paris, he now made the step from arrogant to insufferable.

One day he heard a rumor that Cardinal Mazarin was planning to marry off an Italian niece, Laure Mancini, to the Duc de Mercoeur, a grandson of Henry of Navarre.

Condé found Mazarin in the Louvre, at a reception in one of the long, gallerylike rooms. Before a hundred persons, he grabbed him by the collar of his Cardinal's robe.

"Marry your swarthy little niece to a son of France!" he roared. "You must think you're pretty powerful, you Sicilian rogue!"

Condé hit Mazarin across the face with his open hand as he spoke.

"Take that as the blessing of a gentleman!"

Mazarin laughed.

"Don't get carried away," he said mildly. "The matter hasn't yet been settled."

Condé kept demanding new titles for himself and his

friends, demands that made it clear his ambition knew no limit. Anne and Mazarin tried to put him off with soft answers, waiting for the moment to strike back.

Then Condé went one step too far.

He had the wild idea of finding a lover for the Queen Regent (ignoring Mazarin's considerable claims to that honor). From his own followers he selected a giddy young man called the Marquis de Jarzé. Jarzé tried to make advances, but was brutally put in his place by the Queen. Condé demanded a public apology to his protégé. He got the apology, but it was asking too much. Anne of Austria and Mazarin decided to make their move.

On the morning of January 18, 1650, Anne took young Louis by the hand and led him into her private chapel at the Palais Royal. She told him that she had ordered the arrest of Condé, his brother, and his brother-in-law. Then they both went down on their knees and prayed for the success of the plan.

Later in the morning came the news: Guitaut, captain of the Royal Guards, had picked up Condé, along with the Prince de Conti and the Duc de Longueville, as they arrived at the Palais Royal. At first Condé had thought that Guitaut was joking, but all three had surrendered quietly enough. They were already on their way to prison in the grim old *donjon* at Vincennes.

Anne opened the doors of her private apartments and the Court streamed in to compliment her on the act. Gaston d'Orleans, who always handled a phrase better than a sword, made the neatest comment:

"The lion, the monkey, and the fox–all caught in the same net!"

Paris laughed, lit bonfires, breathed a collective sigh of relief that the wings of the rumpled eagle had been clipped at last.

Inevitably there had been fear beforehand that the arrest of the three would stir up another Fronde. Some steps were taken to keep De Retz from his usual troublemaking. He was even promised his long-desired Cardinal's hat if he would just behave!

Unfortunately, Condé's wife, his mother, and his sister, the Duchesse de Longueville, escaped the net. From outside Paris they started stirring the same old pot of riot and revolt. Turenne, still bewitched, promised to do his best to help, and this time the Frondeurs got a sort of half-hearted agreement from Gaston d'Orleans to join the plot.

The events of the Fronde which followed, called the Fronde of the Princes, scarred young Louis for life.

Fighting flared all over France. Louis took the field with a royal army which overran Burgundy, a province controlled by Condé. The Prince's men entrenched themselves at Bellegarde, and the King's troops promptly surrounded the town.

In that serious, grown-up way of his, young Louis inspected his men. From the ramparts of the town came cheers for the little King, then a volley of musket shots. An officer standing within two feet of Louis fell dead.

Such was his baptism of fire, sadly in civil war. It was a lesson he never forgot. . . .

Later, another revolt flared in the Bordeaux area. Again, Louis joined the troops who were laying siege to the southern city. One night a courtier called Lomenie de Brienne, who was close to the King, found young Louis in tears in his tent.

"What is the matter, dear master? Why do you cry?"

"I won't always be a child," said Louis between sobs. "But don't say anything! I don't want anyone to know about my tears. These Bordeaux rascals won't lay down the law to me much longer!"

The Paris Parlement took the side of the three imprisoned princes, who by now had been moved to Le Havre for safekeeping. The Parlement's President, Molé, came to the Palais Royal bringing a sharp warning to the Queen Regent that they should be released.

Anne of Austria listened carefully, then dismissed Molé with a curt word or two.

As soon as they were alone, Louis, who was twelve by now, spoke up vigorously.

"If I hadn't been afraid of making you angry, Mother, I would have silenced the President, and had him removed three times sooner."

Now, amid all the new tumult, Mazarin—the supple, the ingratiating—lost his touch and his nerve. In the Royal Council he drew an unfortunate comparison between the new Fronde and the forces who had so recently beheaded King Charles of England. This was too much for Gaston d'Orleans, who went over to the rebels as completely as his shifting nature could go over to anything.

Parlement voted the freeing of the princes and the banishment of Mazarin. Just to make the second vote clear, they encouraged the people of Paris to hang Mazarin in effigy, which they did.

Even though the Queen ignored the votes, Mazarin in sudden panic decided to flee. First he disguised himself in the blue-and-silver uniform of a musketeer. Then, taking with him a young clerk called Colbert, some of the crown jewels and not much else, he slipped away, reaching Saint-Germain in safety.

De Retz, who was of course in the forefront of the furor once again, was quite sure that the Queen and young Louis would follow Mazarin as soon as possible. He asked Gaston to order the closing of the city gates. As usual Gaston couldn't make up his mind. His wife gave the command in his name.

All that evening—it was the night of February 9, 1651—De Retz's men stirred up the Paris mob by spreading rumors that Louis and his mother were again planning to leave the capital city (as they were indeed doing).

At two in the morning citizens by the thousand stormed into the courtyard of the Palais Royal, yelling to see their King.

Young Louis was already dressed in riding clothes, booted and spurred for escape. Acting with great spirit, Anne of Austria told him to climb quickly into the royal bed and pull the heavy covers over him.

Then she ordered the palace doors thrown open to the mob. They streamed up the great staircase, along corridors, and galleries until they came to the open door of the royal bedroom.

There the Queen greeted them.

"I had you come," she said, "because I am surrounded with enemies and only feel safe when I am in your midst."

"We were told you were planning to leave tonight,"

one of the crowd called out. "And that the King is already dressed to go. Is this true?"

In answer she stood aside. The crowd surged into the room.

"Quiet!" she called, doing her best to keep her voice from going shrill. "The King, my son, sleeps."

More subdued now, the people of Paris moved past the bed where Louis lay pretending to be asleep. One citizen soldier parted the curtains with his pike. From then on everyone had a good close look.

The sight of their small, sleeping King calmed the people. For hours butchers and bargemen, merchants and tailors, fishwives, housewives, coopers, beggars, gaolers trooped by the bed. By invitation of the Queen, two of their number stood watch.

Angry, not a little frightened, almost stifling in his heavy riding clothes, young Louis pretended to sleep on.

13. OF CODES AND CAVALCADES

Mazarin saw that for the moment the game was lost. With the Queen and young Louis virtual prisoners in the Palais Royal, there was only one thing to do to ensure their safety and his own: free the three princes.

He rode posthaste to Le Havre, arriving at the castle just as Condé, Conti, and Longueville were sitting down to dinner. He told them that the Queen had ordered that they be released at once. Condé, who knew how to behave like a prince when he was in the mood, gravely asked the Cardinal to join them for supper. The meal passed in civilized fashion. Then Condé's carriage was called, Mazarin accompanied the Prince and his two kinsmen to the courtyard.

One report says that Mazarin kissed Condé's boot as he entered the carriage, but this may have been going too far even for the smooth, ingratiating Italian. We do know that Condé gave him the curtest of nods in farewell, flung himself into the carriage, and ordered his coachmen to whip up the horses. With a burst of laughter that echoed in the stone courtyard the captives drove across the lowered drawbridge and into freedom.

Mazarin himself kept right on going–putting as many miles as possible between himself, the princes, and the Paris mob. He rode north and east and didn't stop until he crossed the German border. Finally he took refuge at a manor house near Cologne.

The Parlement wasted no time in pillaging the wealth and property which the Prime Minister left behind. His splendid fifty-four-thousand-volume library was sacked, his castles and town house sold, and his art collection–one of the finest in Europe–distributed to his "creditors," who turned up by the score.

Shocked by the luxury in which Mazarin had lived, the fickle Paris public welcomed Condé back with glee. The flaring torches that had celebrated his imprisonment a few months before now burned more brightly than ever.

Gaston d'Orleans had become Regent in all but name, and his advisers were urging him to depose Anne and take over. But Condé brushed him aside like a stray moth. Everybody turned to the victor of Rocroi as the man of the hour, and the man for the years to come. He grew more arrogant by the day.

Condé even snubbed his cousin the King.

On July 31, 1651, as on most days, young Louis went for a swim in the Seine. As he and a few friends were riding back to the palace along the Cours-la-Reine, Condé came bowling along in his open carriage, with a mounted escort.

Seeing the King, Condé waved casually. In those times when the King passed, even a Prince of the Blood stopped his carriage, climbed out, bowed very low indeed. So this was more than a studied insult–it was a kind of sacrilege.

Louis went pale with anger.

"If I had had my guards with me," he said when he reached the palace, "I would have given *Monsieur le Prince* a real scare."

From his manor house in Germany, Mazarin continued to exert his influence over the Queen Regent.

Mazarin's famous letters in code date from this time. Almost every day mounted couriers carried them from Germany to Paris. Here are some typical excerpts:

> I close by assuring you that the sea is not calm nor the sky serene, and that the Serafin is the cause, but 46 will always be faithful, zealous and passionate in his service of. . . .

The star was the agreed symbol for Mazarin's love of Anne. *Sea* and *sky* were two of the words Mazarin used in referring to himself. He also used the numbers 26 and 46. *Serafin* was one of his names for Anne. Since it was a masculine name, some slight confusion was added.

> I have just seen a letter of Serafin written to 46 which ends in the most agreeable fashion one could imagine: for *he* says that if *he* were dying his last thought would be
>
> ‡

This symbol stood for the Queen's love of Mazarin. Often, at the end of her own rather childish letters to Mazarin, she would scrawl it all over the bottom of the page—more like a schoolgirl than a widow in her forties.

Mazarin had advice for the Queen down to the most minute details of government, and never failed to remind her of his own love and his own usefulness. Here is one more example, warning her against a member of the Royal Council called Chavigny. This time the agreed code words were *Zabaot* for the Queen, and both 26 and 46 for Mazarin:

> Remember that 57 [Chavigny] is only working for the destruction of all that Zabaot loves best. I think therefore that Zabaot should take great heed to the counsels of 46 not only on account of the affection *he* bears toward him but because in things both past and present 26 is far more intelligent than those now in command.

Mazarin in exile never gave up his loyalty to France. When the Emperor Leopold tried to win him over to the Hapsburg cause, he wrote quite nobly in reply: "I will end my days as a servant of France–in my thoughts and through my hopes if I can do so in no other way."

As it turned out, Mazarin did not have to languish long in Germany.

In September 1651 young Louis became thirteen, the traditional age for a king of France to attain his majority. With Paris and all France in turmoil, it was decided that a great and impressive spectacle might have a calming effect.

At eight o'clock on the morning of September 7, Louis left the Palais Royal for the Île de la Cité and the *lit de justice* he would hold there.

His escort was superb.

A troop of light cavalry led the parade. Then came a group of the first noblemen in France. The governors of the provinces were next, followed by the members of the Order of the Holy Spirit.

Then there marched the Gentlemen of the Royal Bedchamber and the Grand Officers of the King.

Six royal trumpeters, making silvery sounds in the morning air, were succeeded by six heralds on horseback, then the Marshals of France (all but the Great Condé, who was sulking at Chantilly).

Then, all alone, came the Comte d'Harcourt, the Master of the Royal Horse. He carried the King's own sword in its blue velvet scabbard, sprinkled with the golden lilies of France.

Then, hats in hand, plumes sweeping the ground, came the royal pages, the valets . . . the foot soldiers of the palace guard . . . the ushers and mace-bearers.

Last of all rode young Louis on a cream-colored Arab horse. His cloak gleamed with gold and precious stones, and the Order of the Holy Spirit hung on its blue ribbon at his throat.

He was so big for his age, so strong and kingly, that he made an impression no one who saw him ever forgot. It was really the beginning of the legend of the Sun King—the symbol he would later adopt as his own. For, according to the testimony of many spectators, it almost seemed as if rays of majesty came from him as he rode through the packed streets.

At the high Gothic portal of the Sainte-Chapelle, young Louis was received by the Bishop of Bayeux and other ranking churchmen. After taking part in a solemn mass, he walked across to the Palais de Justice where the Parlement awaited him.

"Gentlemen," said Louis in his clear young voice, "I have come to tell you that in accordance with the law of my state, I am going to take upon myself the management of my government, and I hope that God will grant that this will be done with piety and with justice."

The Queen then relinquished to him her powers as Regent. Embracing his mother, Louis said:

"Madam, I thank you for the care that you have been pleased to take for my education and for the governing of my kingdom. I pray you to go on giving me of your wisdom, and I wish to see you, after me, as the Chief of my Council."

As a first matter of business, a court official announced three Royal Edicts: one against dueling, another against swearing, and a third offering a full pardon to the great and rebellious Condé.

Then everyone from the Duc d'Anjou to the Officers of the crown took the solemn oath of loyalty to the new king.

The Great Condé had sent a letter by his brother Conti, asking to be excused from the ceremony. It went unopened. Anne of Austria was furious at this new example of Condé's insolence.

"I will perish, or Monsieur le Prince will!" she screamed.

Shortly afterward, Condé headed south to raise an army and to establish direct contact with Spain. With the King's majority, such acts became high treason.

But there was no turning back for the Prince. To the Frondeurs who were urging him on—his troublemaking sister, his brother Conti, the melancholy La Rochefoucauld, and the rest—he said, "You have forced me to draw my sword against my will; you will see that I will be the last to return it to the scabbard."

14. CANNONS ON THE CAUSEWAY

Young Louis' ceremonial coming-of-age brought no great changes with it. The truth was that he was not yet ready to rule. Although his bearing and manners were very grown up, there was nothing particularly brilliant or precocious about his mind. (Later, Mazarin was to remark that Louis was a slow starter but that he would go further than most.)

So the Queen Regent went on governing pretty much as before–and being governed in turn and from afar by her beloved Mazarin. She was playing for time, for she knew that the latest Fronde–an uncertain alliance of rebellious princes and an ambitious Parlement–couldn't last forever. The moment was sure to come when she would summon her Cardinal back from exile.

She concealed her purpose skillfully, even agreeing to a parliamentary edict condemning the fugitive Prime Minister to perpetual exile as an enemy of the state. In this dissembling, young Louis was a great help to her, for he was grave and courteous to everyone, and by now very adroit at concealing his own feelings.

Certain events began to favor the royal cause.

First of all, Turenne's infatuation for Madame de Longueville suddenly ended. He came back to the side of King and Queen Mother, bringing his mercurial older brother, the Duc de Bouillon, along with him.

This was a serious blow to the Frondeurs. It meant that Turenne and Condé, the two most brilliant generals of their age—who together might well have swept everything before them—were pitted against each other. In effect they canceled each other out.

Also, early in 1652 De Retz received his Cardinal's hat at last. He calmed down almost at once. Instead of continuing in the role of troublemaker-in-chief, he became a slightly erratic supporter of the monarchy.

The Fronde still had to burn itself out. Its final blaze was the gaudiest and most dangerous conflagration of all.

In the spring of 1652 Anne of Austria and young Louis joined the small army which was trying to run Condé to earth. At first everything went well. Free of Paris, excited by one or two small victories, the Queen began to yearn for Mazarin. Both she and Louis wrote him warm letters urging his return. As an even better inducement, the Marshal d'Hocquincourt, a strong Mazarin man, raised eight thousand troops and placed them at the Cardinal's disposal. Mazarin promptly recrossed the border and hurried south to join Anne and Louis.

His return was enough to set the Fronde ablaze. Fused again by their hatred of the Italian, all the disparate forces closed ranks for war.

All that month of March Turenne and Condé stalked each other. Turenne maneuvered under one serious handicap: he was forced by Mazarin's gratitude to Marshal d'Hocquincourt to share command of the royal troops with the Marshal, a soldier of very modest ability.

On the night of April 6, at a town called Bléneau north of the Loire, Condé surprised D'Hocquincourt's forces and cut them to pieces. Turenne viewed the masterly attack from too far away to help, and then saw the camp of his unlucky colleague being put to the torch.

"Ah," he remarked, "I see M. le Prince is there himself. Only he could have carried out that operation."

Now Turenne and some four thousand men were all that stood between Condé's twelve thousand and the King. It looked as if Louis, his mother, and the rest of the Court, who were some miles south of Gien, were sure to be captured.

In that calm way of his, Turenne made his dispositions. First he placed his infantry in a heavily wooded area that lay across Condé's path. Behind the timberland stretched some marshland, and across the marshland ran one narrow causeway. Turenne placed his artillery farther to the rear so that its fire could be concentrated on the causeway.

When, predictably, the outnumbered royal infantry gave ground and scattered under the Prince's onslaught, Condé and his cavalry rode right on through and went thundering down the narrow causeway.

Halfway across, Turenne's cavalry countercharged, absorbing and blunting the headlong attack. Condé's horsemen churned around, with many of their mounts rearing and falling into the marsh to right and left. At exactly the moment of turmoil, Turenne's artillery opened up, tearing great holes in the packed mass of cavalrymen and horses.

It was too much, even for Condé's dashing veterans. They withdrew in some disorder.

Lacking the manpower for a full pursuit, Turenne fell back to higher ground and a good defensive position.

That night, Condé invited the officer commanding Turenne's rear guard to join him for supper.

"What a pity that fine fellows like you and me cut each other's throats over such a scoundrel," the Prince remarked in the most friendly way. The "scoundrel" of course was Mazarin, whom Condé could never think of as anything but an upstart foreign adventurer.

Blocked at Bléneau in his attempt to capture King and Court, Condé now turned and headed north for Paris, so that he could at least control the capital city.

15. THE FRONDE IN FRENZY

At this point the Great Mademoiselle–Anne Marie-Louise d'Orleans, Duchesse de Montpensier, to use her less familiar name–had her moment in history. Anne was twenty-five by now, a big blonde amazon of a woman with fine blue eyes, a good figure, and that outsize Bourbon nose inherited from her grandfather, Henry of Navarre. Although considered as a possible queen by half the crowned heads of Europe, she still dreamed of marrying Louis, the "petit mari" of childhood days. By her own giddy reasoning, she figured that the best way to make her dear cousin marry her would be to build up the Fronde as much as possible. Then, when domestic peace came at last to France, it would be cemented by a marriage between members of the two warring factions!

The trouble was that her father, Gaston, had joined the Fronde in his usual shifty, shiftless way, and only because he hated Mazarin more than he hated his cousin Condé. Anne knew that she would have to take matters into her own hands.

Here is how she came to do so.

Pillaging as he went, Condé—with a demoralized army reduced to five thousand men—reached the suburbs of Paris. On his heels came Turenne, well reinforced, anxious to settle the issue once and for all.

July 2 was the crucial day. Condé had drawn up his forces just outside one of the city gates called the Porte Saint-Antoine. There, behind light entrenchments, he planned to make his stand. Inside the city, the situation was growing more and more confused. Fearing plunder, suspicious of the presence of Spanish troops in Condé's ranks, the officials of the City Council refused to open the gates to the beleaguered army.

Condé had heard that Gaston d'Orleans was ill. Early in the morning he sent a messenger direct to Anne, saying that Turenne's forces were closing in and that he needed permission to enter the city if the day went badly.

Anne was in a state of high excitement. All night long she had heard the throb of drums and bugles under her windows. Now as day broke came the distant rattle of musket fire.

She hurried to the Luxembourg Palace where her father lived. To her surprise she found Gaston up and about.

"I heard you were ill!" she cried. "I expected to find you in bed."

"I am not ill enough to be in bed," Gaston answered sulkily. "But I am too ill to go out."

Weeping with shame, Anne begged him either to jump on a horse and join the defenders or climb back into bed and at least seem to be sick.

Gaston shrugged, bored and indifferent.

Finally Anne and some of the noblemen of the Fronde

persuaded her father to draft a letter to the Council ordering them to help Condé by opening the Paris gates. Carrying the letter, Anne hurried to the Hôtel de Ville through streets thronged with running guardsmen and anxious citizens. There the members of the Council read Gaston's letter carefully, then agreed to send some city militia *out* to help Condé.

"But if the enemy beats the Prince, they'll give Paris no quarter!" Anne cried.

"You know perfectly well, Mademoiselle, that if your troops hadn't approached the city, the royal troops wouldn't have come here either," a grave old councilman answered.

"You're splitting hairs while the Prince is in peril! You can give him help, so do so quickly!" Anne stormed.

Instead, the Council went into a secret session to disuss the problem. Wild with impatience, Anne waited by an open window, half-hearing the sounds of mass from a nearby church. . . .

From the hill of Charonne, where the famous cemetery of Père-Lachaise now is, young Louis and Mazarin watched the battle. By nine o'clock the day was already hot. To them, Turenne's maneuvering seemed maddeningly slow. They ordered him to attack more boldly. Turenne replied that he was waiting for his artillery to come up so that he could first soften up the entrenchments. But now, without waiting for the guns to come up, he moved to the attack.

Soon the battle was fiercely joined, at very close quarters. Much of it was hand-to-hand combat in the old medieval manner, knight against knight, steel against cold steel. Pistol and harquebus fired at almost point-blank range were more modern notes in the crashing symphony.

Barricade by barricade, house by house, garden by garden, the white-scarfed royal troops pushed the Frondeurs back toward the city walls.

Condé was everywhere–hacking, cursing, probing for weakness, loving every desperate moment. Later Turenne paid tribute to his great rival: "I did not see one Condé," he said, "I saw at least a dozen."

Toward noon the intense heat caused a spontaneous truce. Condé stripped to the skin, then rolled in some tall grass along the roadside like a horse. Many of his men just lay and looked at the sky for a while. Some leaned wearily on their swords or pikes and kept a sharp eye on the foe.

After the lull, Condé's cavalry made a desperate charge to break the iron ring that was closing around them. The charge was stopped dead, and the Duc de la Rochefoucauld, one of its leaders, was blinded by a musket shot.

Watching from their hill, young Louis and Mazarin began to hope that the end was near. By now the royal artillery was in action at last, and the raking fire of the great guns was forcing the Frondeurs to take refuge in the shallow moat below the city walls.

Suddenly the Porte Saint-Antoine swung open, and the drawbridge was lowered. Condé's battered troops began to stream across to safety.

Anne's vehemence had saved the day. When it was clear that the danger was lessening, Condé himself entered the city. He was told that his savior was at a house near the Bastille, very close to the city gate. He hurried there to thank her. In her memoirs, Anne has left us a vivid picture of the prince in this extreme moment:

> He had dust two inches thick on his face. His hair was matted, his clothes bloody and torn, though he was himself unwounded; his cuirass was dented with blows and he held his naked sword in his hand.

Even in this crisis Condé observed the etiquette of the time, Anne reported approvingly: he handed his sword to one of her pages. For a moment he gave in to despair, sobbing for all his good friends who had been killed or wounded.

Anne spoke words of comfort, and his intrepid spirit soon came back. At her urging, he dashed into the rearguard action again to make sure all his men got safely across the drawbridge.

Outside the city gate he found that Turenne was now pressing very hard indeed, in a pincers movement that would soon cut off many of the Frondeurs.

Young Louis and the Cardinal, dismayed by the opening of the city gate, began to hope again for a real victory.

Suddenly, as they watched, the cannon on the battlemented towers of the Bastille belched smoke and flame in a rippling volley. Mazarin, who had bribed one of the officers in the old fortress, thought his man had taken over.

"Good," he said. "They're firing on the enemy."

"They seem to be firing on us," one observer chimed in.

Someone suggested that it might be a salute in honor of the Great Mademoiselle, who was believed to be in the city.

"If Mademoiselle is there, you can be sure they're firing on us," said old Marshal Villeroy, who knew Anne well.

As they watched, a whole file of Turenne's crack cavalry

disintegrated. Some of the spent cannonballs from the guns of the Bastille fell at the feet of the royal party.

Now, while the brutal volleys made Turenne's men seek cover in their turn, the last column of rebels fled into the city, and the drawbridge was raised.

"Those cannon," said Mazarin, "have just killed Mademoiselle's husband."

It was quickly known that Anne had ordered the Bastille guns moved across the parapet from their usual position commanding the city streets, and that she herself had given the signal to fire. So Mazarin's cynical remark was right on target. After such open defiance of the King she could never hope, even in her wildest dreams, to be his bride.

Two days after the battle at the city gate, Condé made a crude attempt to seize power. A riot developed, and a near-massacre, in which thirty citizens lost their lives. There was no longer one Fronde but many fragmented elements. Some Parisians supported Gaston. Many were, as always, for the King, provided Mazarin went into exile again. Even the now-passive De Retz had some vestigial followers; many noblemen and a lot of hard-bitten soldiers were loyal to Condé.

The truth was that the terrible four years had almost worn themselves out. The French were sick to death of the Fronde. They were beginning to realize that a strong monarchy was better than endless bloodshed and senseless revolt.

Events moved fast. Mazarin made a perfunctory gesture of exiling himself again for a few months in the interests of peace; but he came back for good early the following year.

On October 21, 1652, young Louis reentered Paris on

horseback, to the wild cheering of his people. This time he made the Louvre his palace rather than the more-exposed Palais Royal, having learned that a good deep moat around one's dwelling has certain very real advantages.

At the gates of the Louvre, Cardinal de Retz welcomed Louis in the name of the Church. But Louis had had enough of the intriguer, placating as De Retz now seemed. A few weeks later, he had him arrested just to be on the safe side.

Gaston and his daughter went into separate exile and La Rochefoucauld joined his wife in the country, where his vision and good sense soon came back. Condé went over to the Spanish Hapsburgs and served them for seven years, fulfilling his prophecy that he would be the last to sheath his sword.

Perhaps because he was the symbol of the terrible, motiveless madness of the Fronde, De Retz should have the final word. In his famous recollections he described the end of a typical day of barricades-and-rioting:

> They dispersed the sooner, because it was suppertime; for you must know that the people of Paris, even those that are the busiest in all such commotions, do not care to lose their meals.

Now all France was ready for her supper.

PART III

THE SUN GOES UP THE SKY

16. THE LEGEND OF THE DIVINE DOVE

The coronation of young Louis would have normally followed his coming-of-age. But the turbulent years of the Fronde forced its postponement. During the year 1653, a desultory campaign against Condé and his new Hapsburg masters, fought mostly in northern France, caused the ceremony to be put off again.

By 1654, with the scars of the Fronde healing fast and the war going well, it was time to crown Louis and so to make him the heir of the great mystical tradition which was his.

Ever since the twelfth century, the kings of France had been crowned at the ancient city of Reims, which lies north and east of Paris. The ritual itself went back to the dim beginnings of the nation's history.

In A.D. 486 Clovis, a bold chieftain of the tribe called the Franks, defeated the Romans at Soissons and drove them out of France. Ten years later he was locked in a desperate battle with the German tribes from across the Rhine. Finding that his pleas to his own pagan gods went unanswered, Clovis swore a mighty oath that he would turn Christian if the tide of combat turned in his favor.

According to a chronicle of the time, the Germans fled

as soon as the Frankish chief swore his oath. Two years later Clovis and some three thousand of his long-haired warriors were baptized by Saint-Remi, bishop of Reims.

By ending the Roman rule, by uniting the French tribes and beating off the Germans, Clovis became the first king of France. He was the only Christian king in the western world. So France, from the very start, was the direct inheritor of the Church of Rome, the "eldest daughter" of Mother Church.

As time passed, baptism and coronation became inseparably linked. By the twelfth century, the story of the baptism of Clovis had grown even more colorful. Now it went like this: just as Saint-Remi was saying a prayer over Clovis, who knelt waist-deep in the water of the big baptismal font, a dove "whiter than snow" flew straight down from heaven. In its beak it carried a glass vial, or flask, about the size of a fig. The vial held a mixture of oil and aromatic balm with which Saint-Remi promptly anointed the convert.

As the legend hardened into history, the ceremony of coronation became a restaging of this divine conversion. On the day of the ritual, the legendary glass vial itself, preserved in a reliquary which was in turn encased in a gold-and-jeweled box, rested on the high altar of the Cathedral.

Down the centuries there remained some reddish sediment in the vial. A particle of this sediment, extracted by a golden needle and mixed with holy oil, was used to anoint each succeeding King of France.

So the King really did rule by divine right. The "Very Christian King" received his power direct from heaven.

One other point shows how closely King and Church were linked from the beginning: Clovis' own emblem was a toad. But he changed it to the stylized, three-pronged cross which we know as the fleur-de-lis. It seems that an angel had appeared to his wife and said this change would increase his prowess on the field of battle. So even the royal banner bearing the golden lilies of France was divine in origin and Christian in design.

On the evening of June 5, 1654, the Court arrived at Reims. Young Louis had his first glimpse of the cathedral by moonlight—like the ghost of all Gothic cathedrals in the clear spring night.

He was lodged at the palace of the archbishops of Reims. At six o'clock on the morning of June 7, the Bishop of Beauvais, in his full pontifical splendor, tapped on his door with a silver wand.

"Whom do you want?" the Lord Chamberlain asked from within.

"We want the King."

"The King is asleep."

The dialogue was repeated three times; then the Bishop added these words:

"We seek Louis, the Fourteenth of that name, son of the great King Louis XIII, whom God has given us as King."

The door opened to reveal Louis lying on his state bed with his eyes closed. He wore a red satin tunic trimmed with gold and a diamond-studded cap of black velvet with a white plume.

The Bishop presented a silver bowl with holy water in it. Opening his eyes as if from sleep, Louis dipped his fingers in the water and made the sign of the cross, while the Bishop prayed.

Then Louis joined the procession that was waiting at the

palace gates to escort him to the cathedral.

It was a fine, sunny day. The streets were lined with the people of the city.

Once inside, Louis walked down the long nave to the choir and knelt at a desklike stand called a prie-dieu just below the high altar.

Every seat on the floor of the cathedral and in its high galleries was full. The royal family, the Princes of the Blood, the Twelve Dukes and Peers of the realm, nobles and commoners from the four corners of France formed the congregation.

First, Louis made a solemn promise in Latin to defend and observe the rights of the Catholic Church.

Then the Bishop of Soissons, who was officiating, asked the congregation if they would accept the Prince as King. The question was greeted by the deep silence of approval.

Now Louis in a strong voice spoke the coronation oath.

"I make this promise to the Christian people, and my subjects, in the name of Christ. . . ."

He promised that his government would maintain the true peace of God, that he would prohibit all violence and acts of injustice, and that he would enjoin equity and mercy to be used in all judgments and so "earn the favor for himself and his people of a merciful and gracious God."

The Lord Chamberlain slipped shoes of violet velvet on Louis' feet, and the Duc d'Anjou knelt and attached the golden spurs.

The Bishop of Soissons blessed the King's sword, known as Joyeuse (because it was only produced on days of joy). Louis kissed the blade and raised it high as an offering to God.

The sword was passed to the Constable of France, who held it, blade pointing toward heaven, for the rest of the ceremony.

Now came the most sacred part of all.

To show his utter humility before the awesome inheritance that would soon be his, Louis lay face downward on a strip of velvet.

Meanwhile, the Bishop approached the high altar where the reliquary of Saint-Remi had been placed. From it he drew a drop of the heavenly balm. Then he took a golden chalice and mixed the balm with holy oil.

A long chanting of litanies followed, while Louis continued to lie prone.

Finally Louis rose and knelt before the Bishop. After dipping his thumb into the chalice, the Bishop anointed Louis in seven places: on brow and chest, between the shoulders, on right shoulder and left, at bend of right arm and bend of left.

Louis was then dressed in royal vestments very similar to those of a high churchman. The Bishop anointed him twice more, making the sign of the cross on the palm of each hand.

Next, the symbols of his sovereign powers were presented to him—the six-foot scepter and the gold-and-ivory hand of justice.

Finally, the Bishop placed the crown of Charlemagne upon his head. It was already more than eight hundred years old, a helmet of beaten gold with only a few jewels showing. It was so unadorned that it had its own impressiveness. Few present were unaware of what the crown symbolized—for with it Charlemagne had been made Em-

peror of the West by the Pope himself, ruler of the Low Countries, Austria and a good deal of Italy and Germany as well as of France.

On the thousand-year-old throne of King Dagobert, Louis received homage from the Peers of the Realm, who each in turn kissed his cheek.

"May the King live forever!" the Bishop intoned.

As hundreds of birds were released from the galleries, the west doors of the cathedral were thrown open. Outside, the King's guards fired three volleys so that the city would know that the consecration and the crowning had truly taken place.

There was more ritual to come. Mass was celebrated. The King went to confession and received Communion. At last, wearing a light crown of pearls and diamonds now, he walked down the central aisle to jubilant organ notes and the boom of the cathedral bells.

Outside, in the sunlit square, the people had been waiting patiently hour after hour to see their new King.

Now at last they saw him, and they liked what they saw.

They liked his splendid bearing and the vigor that he radiated. The mild eye of the boy-man of fifteen, the already sensual mouth were balanced by the fine, bold Bourbon nose and the firm jaw. The abundant dark-brown hair made him seem taller than his medium height.

They saw him as many kinds of king. He was now the Lord's anointed and as such himself almost a demigod. He was their champion against the nobles, their leader in battle. He was the healer of the sick and the embodiment of their fair land of France.

"*Vive le roi*!" they thundered, and thundered again, cheer on deep-throated cheer.

17. APPRENTICE KING

Right after his coronation, young Louis—having just promised to maintain the true peace of God—went off to war again. It was clear that if there was ever going to be *any* kind of peace, heavenly or earth-bound, it would have to come with a decisive victory over the Great Condé.

With Turenne as his teacher, Louis was learning a lot about the art of war. His days were spent in the saddle and his nights under canvas.

During that summer of 1654, four key towns in succession fell to the royal army—Rethel, Sedan, Stenay, and Arras.

At one point, Condé's Spanish troops did win a minor skirmish and captured a few French battle flags. Perhaps a little embarrassed at seeing his own family fleur-de-lis on the flags, Condé promptly returned the standards to his cousin Louis. Young Louis sent them right back again with a polite note. Since Condé captured so few French flags these days, Louis suggested that he keep those he did manage to take!

An unkind critic once remarked that Louis XIV's love of war was mainly a fondness for laying siege to almost undefended towns.

This was most unfair. Louis loved the handling of edged weapons and all the manly skills of horsemanship. He loved the delicate and precise art of artillery and the organized confusion of battle.

In temperament, Louis had always been more Turenne's cautious man than Condé's bold one. So he and the steady, sturdy Marshal (anxious to prove what a loyal subject he had become again) worked very well together in double harness.

By now, another splendid soldier was beginning to make his name. This was Sébastien Vauban, a most remarkable engineer. Vauban revolutionized the whole science of fortification and siege warfare. He studied angles of fire as no man ever had before, and was the first to realize that a ricocheting bullet or cannonball could have great effect. In all, 333 forts and fortified towns were touched by his genius. The low, star-shaped citadels which he built can still be seen all over Europe.

Vauban was an architect as well as an engineer. His use of stone and brick and mortar, in massive and elegant harmony, has rarely been equaled.

Vauban also invented the bayonet. Up to his time, soldiers simply rammed a specially designed dagger or short sword into the muzzle of their muskets for close combat. Vauban slung the dagger *under* the barrel, attaching it by a steel sleeve so that the musket could either fire or thrust. The arsenal at Bayonne in southern France turned out these businesslike weapons by the thousand, which is why they came to be known as bayonets.

In due course Louis made Vauban a marquis and a marshal of France. And, a hundred years after the death of the great engineer, Napoleon moved his tomb to the Invalides chapel, where he is enshrined among some of the most famous soldiers of France.

Young Louis turned sixteen in September. He had the good sense to realize that he was still not ready to rule, and that in Mazarin he had a Prime Minister who was ruling for him very skillfully indeed.

Some historians have maintained that Louis hated his godfather, but this is absolutely false. After the Cardinal's return from exile, their relationship was increasingly warm and close.

When in Paris, they met every day to go over state dispatches. Mazarin saw to it that Louis took part in sessions of the Royal Council—but never so long or so many as to become boring. Then Louis would be off again—to lunch with his mother, to his riding lesson, to hunt or shoot in the nearby forest of Vincennes.

Mazarin was proud of Louis' progress.

"You have the stuff to make four great kings and an honest man besides," he once remarked in his smooth-cynical way.

Not everyone was impressed by Louis' industry. Some of the Court thought he lived only for pleasure. We shall see how badly they underestimated the prodigious machine for governing which was slowly being created.

The nation on the whole was in the mood to be gay, and looked to their fine young king to set the pace. There was a French tradition of public performance by the monarch which Louis willingly revived. He rode, hunted, danced for all to see.

The ballet was a favorite pastime. Young Louis' grace and stamina were much admired. Five times that winter he performed publicly in a ballet called *The Night*, in which he played the part of the rising sun. He wore a golden wig and a costume of flaming rays from head to foot. At one point he recited these words:

A divine hand has given me the reins;
A great goddess has supported my claims.
We share the same glory: she is the star of queens,
I am the star of kings.

Later Louis officially took the sun as his emblem, along with the curious motto, *Nec Pluribus Impar*, which literally means "not unequal to many others." Either Louis liked the double negative, or he had an untypical moment of diffidence.

When the Fronde collapsed, a chastened Parlement had humbly agreed not to interfere in financial matters. Now there was trouble again. Mazarin and Louis needed money for the war. Mazarin's clever Superintendent of Finance, Nicolas Fouquet, came up with some suggestions for new Edicts—seventeen in all—which would bring in the needed funds. Instead of simply rubber-stamping its approval, as it had in the past, the Parlement met in a most critical mood to consider the merit of the Edicts.

Young Louis and Mazarin were hunting in the forest of Vincennes when they heard the news. Spurring his horse, Louis headed straight for the Palais de Justice. He covered most of the four miles at a full gallop. He ran up the steps, burst into the vaulted room where the 220 members in their scarlet robes were sitting in solemn assembly.

The members looked at the young man in amazement. In his high boots and red hunting coat, with a gray hat on his head and a riding crop in his hand, he seemed an intruder and a stranger.

Then he started to speak, and there was no mistaking who he was:

> Everyone knows how much trouble your meetings have caused in my state. . . . I have learnt that you intend to continue them on the pretext of discussing the Edicts which not long since were published and read in my presence. I have come here expressly to forbid you to do this, which I do absolutely. . . .

He strode out again before anyone could say anything in reply.

This scene became the stuff of legends. The most famous is that young Louis cracked his whip and said, "*L'état c'est moi*!"

There is no evidence that he did this. But the underlying intent was certainly there.

The time for a complete takeover had not yet come. Mazarin, the master diplomat, calmed down the members, and the Edicts were passed with almost no dissent.

The year 1657 was spent in campaigning during the

good weather, and in the pleasures of court life during the winter months.

Mazarin and young Louis were more determined than ever to cage the eagle Condé. So they made a treaty with the British Protector, Oliver Cromwell, for joint action against the Spanish Hapsburgs.

The British Commonwealth, already at war with Spain in the New World, agreed to supply six thousand troops to help cut off Dunkirk. This was the Channel harbor which served as chief port of supply for the Spanish Netherlands.

By the end of May 1658 Louis and Turenne had surrounded Dunkirk. A British fleet, lying off the sand dunes, made sure there could be no escape or relief by sea.

Don John of Austria and a Spanish army hurried to the scene to try to raise the siege. Condé was second-in-command. The army took up a position on the sand dunes, with their lines at right angles to the sea.

When Condé, who for once was a little late to arrive on the scene, saw what the Spanish had done, he was not at all pleased.

"Have you ever seen a battle lost?" he asked the young Duke of Gloucester, who was serving under him.

"No, sir," answered the Duke.

"Well, you'll see one now," said the famous soldier.

The reason was obvious to Condé's trained eye. The Spanish had formed their lines at high tide. The steep Channel tide was already beginning to ebb, leaving their right flank exposed.

Turenne launched a sudden cavalry charge across the hardening sand and rolled up the Spanish flank.

At the same time the French infantry and Cromwell's

foot soldiers in their red coats stormed the Spanish center, which was well entrenched in the high dunes.

This was the first appearance of the "redcoats" on the continent of Europe, and their valor began a tradition that soon became a legend.

When their front line, storming up the dunes, slipped in the heavy sand, the men in the second line boosted their comrades with their rifle butts. In turn, the second line was vigorously butted by the third line.

Despite heavy fire and bristling pikes, the British surged irresistibly up and into the Spanish positions. Victory was soon theirs.

The French foot soldiers, in less arduous climbing, also acquitted themselves very well. The Spanish lost thirteen hundred killed and four thousand prisoners.

Such was the celebrated Battle of the Dunes. Ten days later, on June 25, Dunkirk fell, and Louis, at the head of the Anglo-French army, rode triumphantly into the city.

On June 30, he complained of feeling tired. The doctors said he was exhausted from too many hours in the saddle, and that he had a touch of sunstroke as well. They prescribed rest.

As usual, the doctors were wrong. Somewhere along the dank tidal flats around Dunkirk young Louis had picked up a typhoid germ.

Six days later he was dying.

18. SOME ANXIOUS MONTHS

In those days bleeding was the great cure-all. Louis was bled eight times by his eight court doctors.

His temperature rose alarmingly, and he grew steadily weaker.

Cardinal Mazarin was in despair. "It is not only the King my master who is dangerously ill," he wrote, "but . . . the best friend I have in the world."

On the sixth day, plans were made to administer the last rites of the Church. Louis was quite calm and fully aware that his life was in danger.

"You are a man of resolution," he said to Mazarin, "and the best friend I have: therefore alert me when I am near death, for the Queen would not dare to do so for fear of making me worse."

A local doctor was called. Instead of bleedings and violent purges, he proposed that Louis drink three ounces of a certain wine that would make him vomit.

Willing to try any cure, Mazarin and Louis agreed. The King swallowed the wine and threw up violently twice. Soon his fever broke. By the next day he was out of danger.

By the end of July he was making so good a recovery that the Court moved to Compiègne, where the forest air was the purest in France.

During this anxious time, several of Cardinal Mazarin's nieces (of which he had eight) took turns at young Louis' bedside. One of them was seventeen-year-old Marie Mancini, whom Louis had known for years as a family friend and playmate.

Her grief at his suffering was so sincere that Louis took a new look at her, and liked what he saw. When he was past his crisis, she told him with tears in her eyes that if he had died, she would have died too.

With his own robust love of life flooding back, Louis soon had no thoughts but for the Italian girl. Even making war was forgotten.

Young Louis was in love at last.

Marie was the second youngest of quite a troop of "Mazarinettes." Two of the nieces–Anne-Marie and Laure –were the daughters of a sister of the Cardinal who had married a man named Martinozzi. Five were Mancinis– Olympe, another Laure, Hortense, Marie, and Marie-Anne.

Mazarin imported them from Italy in twos and threes to amuse the Court, divert the King, and make dynastic marriages suitable to his own hard-earned grandeur.

They were lively girls, full of temperament, giggles, and tears. They were dark-skinned and very thin, and the French thought them ugly. Here is one contemporary description: "They have the eyes of owls, the eyebrows of lost souls, and the complexions of a chimney."

Our old friend Madame de Motteville focused her own acid comment on Marie: "She was so thin and her arms and neck seemed so long and fleshless that it was impossible to praise her. . . . Her eyes were big and black, but as yet without fire in them." That shrewd observer did grant her fine teeth and a flashing smile.

All the nieces were gay, and Marie seems to have had quite a fatal charm despite her indifferent looks. When she was still a small child, her father, who was dying, had a moment of insight: "Put her in a nunnery," he said, "for she'll cause a lot of trouble if you don't."

Like his famous grandfather, Henry of Navarre, Louis was strongly attracted to women from early youth. As far back as 1651, when he was thirteen, one of the Great Mademoiselle's ladies-in-waiting caught his eye. She was the dazzling and flirtatious Comtesse de Frontenac.

Louis used to join the two ladies for morning rides. The Great Mademoiselle, vain and giddy as always, thought her cousin was seeking her out. But Anne of Austria knew her son better than that. Well aware that Madame de Frontenac was unhappily married and a troublemaker, she forbade Louis to go riding with the two ladies.

Louis lost his temper.

"When I am master," he cried, "I'll go where I please, and I'll soon be!"

Anne burst into tears, Louis sobbed in his turn, and then they patched it all up. There were no more morning rides with the fair Comtesse.

The following year, Louis had a mild flirtation with Olympe Mancini. But when she was quickly married off to the Comte de Soissons, a Prince of the Blood, he scarcely seemed to notice.

Later, just after that surprise visit to the Parlement in his

hunting coat, Louis got a tongue-lashing from his mother over another girl. It seems he had opened a Court ball by dancing with one of the Mancini girls instead of with his little cousin Henrietta of England.

"I don't like skinny little girls," he muttered as Anne of Austria stormed.

Now he liked Marie, grown slender rather than just plain thin. Her hair was a glossy black, her eyes had lost their dullness, and the smile was more enchanting than ever. At Compiègne and later that summer at Fontainebleau, she and Louis were never apart for long. They rode through the open glades of the forest, danced in the great ballroom of the château. Louis played the guitar and even read a few books so he could discuss them with his brilliant Marie.

Cardinal Mazarin and Anne of Austria were in the meantime looking around for a bride for young Louis. For years it had been assumed that he would some day marry his cousin, the Infanta Maria Theresa of Spain, and so bring two great kingdoms together at last.

The fact that the war was still going on made negotiations difficult. In typical fashion, Mazarin reckoned that if they looked elsewhere for a royal bride, the Spaniards would hasten to end the war and agree to the desired marriage.

He and Anne decided that another cousin, the Princess Marguerite of Savoy, would be the most suitable choice. The Dowager Duchess of Savoy—a daughter of Henry of Navarre and so Louis' aunt—was delighted at the prospect. The courts of France and Savoy agreed to meet at Lyons in the fall of 1658 for further discussions. Mazarin made sure that the Spaniards knew exactly what was going on.

No one seems to have thought that Louis' feeling for Marie would upset these plans. Anne and Mazarin may even have felt that a little mild diversion before marrying was not such a bad idea and would help him back to full health. Louis was certainly making a most remarkable recovery.

In the sunshine of a golden October, the Court moved toward Lyons. Inevitably, Marie Mancini went too. She and Louis rode side by side along the Saône and through the Burgundian hills. Sometimes they galloped wildly, sometimes they walked their horses, talking endlessly as they ambled along.

Despite Marie, Louis seems to have been quite interested in meeting Princess Marguerite, and perhaps even resigned to a marriage for reasons of state.

When they reached Lyons and he saw Marguerite for the first time, he was pleasantly surprised.

"Well, my son?" Anne of Austria asked him after the meeting.

"She is very small," he answered, "but she has the prettiest figure in the world. Her complexion is a sort of olive, but it suits her. She has beautiful eyes. She's just the kind of girl I like."

Marie pointed out that her nose was shapeless and she had those heavy Bourbon cheeks.

"Aren't you ashamed that they should want you to have such a homely wife?" she asked him.

For her part, the little Savoyard princess found her cousin Louis most amiable. They rode in his carriage together, and he told her about his troops and the campaigns he had taken part in. She proved a good listener.

Everyone seemed quite pleased with the way things were going except Anne of Austria, who had set her heart on the Spanish marriage. Even Mazarin seemed content to have Louis drift into marrying Marguerite. At least he refused to show his hand.

Suddenly all was changed. One of Mazarin's confidential agents slipped into Lyons from Madrid in disguise. After talking to him, the Cardinal hurried to the disconsolate Queen Mother.

"Good news, Madame!" he said in a low voice.

"What news could be good save news of peace with Spain?"

"I bring you better news even than that. I come to announce to your Majesty peace *and* the Infanta."

No one knows exactly when Louis and Marie fell hopelessly in love, but they did. Certainly, it was after the negotiations with Savoy were broken off, and poor little Marguerite was left to brood over the handsome cousin who had almost been hers.

Perhaps it was the sure knowledge that he would soon be married to someone he had never seen that made Louis begin to cherish every hour with Marie.

Marie encouraged him to be his own master, and found him more than willing.

"I will never marry the Infanta!" he swore. "You will be my queen. If I want you, who can prevent it?"

Louis tried out the idea of marrying Marie on his mother. His argument was ingenious: He and Anne both owed so much to their Prime Minister that making his niece queen was only fair.

Anne of Austria was seriously alarmed and of course went straight to Mazarin. For one wild moment the Italian was tempted by the dream of having his niece Queen of France. But he loved Louis more than he loved Marie, and France better than his own glory.

Soon he and Anne were plotting how to break up the hopeless love affair.

First of all the pair had to be physically separated. They ordered Louis to Chantilly, north of Paris, and Marie to a lonely little seaport-citadel called Brouage, below La Rochelle on the Atlantic coast.

Both, surprisingly, went quietly enough. There were overtones of tragedy in the parting scene, but also something charadelike.

The King saw his beloved to her coach, which was waiting in the courtyard of the Louvre. They fell into each other's arms, both weeping.

Marie had her last line ready:

"You love me, you are the King–you weep, yet I must go!"

She threw herself into the coach, sobbing wildly that she had been abandoned. The coach clattered across the drawbridge and away.

Louis stood for a long time watching as the coach grew small.

19. THE ISLAND IN THE RIVER

The Bidassoa River is short as rivers go. It curves down through the foothills of the western Pyrenees for sixty miles or so and empties into the Bay of Biscay. But it plays a role far greater than its modest length. For, during the lower part of its course, it serves as the boundary of France and Spain.

Near its mouth there is a small island called the Île des Faisans. The island sits on the thread of the river—the central dividing line—so that it lies half in Spain and half in France. Today it is overgrown with scrub oak and hardly ever visited, even by the pheasants for whom it was named. But in the sixteenth and seventeenth centuries the island was quite famous. It was the "anti-chamber of France," where the French and their ancestral enemy to the south could meet, confer, exchange prisoners with no loss of face to either warring party.

Here, starting in July 1659, Mazarin and the Spanish Prime Minister, Don Luis de Haro, negotiated for five long months. It was their job to hammer out the peace which both countries wanted, and to agree on the terms of the marriage which would make the peace valid and real.

The wooden building in which they met was just about as wide as the little island itself. Covered galleries, held up by boats moored in the river, led to the shores of the two countries.

Each of the prime ministers had his own desk and chair. Mazarin sat in France under an elegant Gobelin tapestry. Two feet away sat Don Luis in Spain, under a more somber Andalusian scene.

After losing the Battle of the Dunes, Spain was not in a very strong bargaining position. Don Luis was every bit as smooth and subtle as Mazarin, with just as much steel under the velvet. But the Cardinal held certain trump cards and played them very well indeed.

One trump was his knowledge that Spain was bankrupt. So he asked the not unreasonable sum of five hundred thousand golden écus as dowry for the Infanta, part of which was to be paid on the wedding day. Out of Spanish pride, Don Luis agreed.

Mazarin then casually suggested that some form of compensation might be in order if the payments weren't made on time. One condition for the marriage had been that Maria Theresa should renounce all her claims to Spanish possessions. With a weather eye on the rich Spanish Netherlands, Mazarin threw in a casual suggestion. In the unlikely event that the dowry wasn't forthcoming, perhaps she should retain these rights?

Don Luis agreed.

This low-key agreement ultimately became Article Two of the treaty, and in time had a powerful effect on the map of Europe.

Another article concerned the fate of the Great Condé. The Spanish were determined that he should not be made to suffer for his service in their ranks and his treason to France. After an exchange of letters with Louis, Mazarin finally agreed on a full pardon, but drove a shrewd bargain. In return, France got four cities in Flanders, five fortified border towns, and a good share of the Belgian province of Hainaut. This was in addition to Roussillon and most of Artois, which had been conceded from the start.

After their parting in the Louvre courtyard, both young Louis and Marie went into paroxysms of loneliness and remorse. They wrote each other every day. At Chantilly Louis read her letters over and over again and lived only for another meeting. Marie mooned along the battlements at Brouage and watched the Atlantic rollers come combing in.

While journeying south for his meeting with Don Luis, Mazarin wrote a series of letters to his godson which are astonishing in their firmness and candor. Again and again he reverted to the same theme: the King's *gloire* and the great future that was in store for him must not be sacrificed: "It is not a question of your desires. . . . Your subjects' welfare and your kingdom are at stake."

As usual, Mazarin threatened to go on his travels if Louis persisted in his fatal passion. Listen to him, pounding away on his favorite theme: "God established kings to guarantee the good, the security, and the peace of their subjects, and not to sacrifice these goods and that peace for their own individual passions."

Poor Louis! At heart he knew the game of love was lost.

He just wanted to see his black-haired, black-eyed Marie once more. His mother, who was suffering too, was sympathetic to this forlorn little wish.

The chance came in mid-August. Louis was journeying south in a ten-month royal progress which would end with his wedding to Maria Theresa down on the Spanish border. At the crossroads town of Saint-Jean d'Angély, which is near Brouage in the pleasant region called the Charente, he and Marie met for the last time.

Marie, whose allowance had been cut to almost nothing by her uncle, wore a simple gray dress with just a touch of lace at the throat and cuffs. She and Louis spent an innocent evening holding hands, gazing long and fondly into each other's eyes, hoping for some reprieve. But the tides of their separate fates were already pulling them apart.

In the morning Louis gave Marie a favorite puppy of his called Friponne, and they embraced one last time. Then he galloped south down the white roads of the Charente, and she went back to her lonely exile.

Today Brouage is sadder than ever. The ocean has receded, so that the little walled town seems to be stranded in the salt marshes some miles from the sea. You can still walk along the ramparts just as Marie did. If you can raise him, a lone guide will show you the small white house where she cried through the long nights.

Finally, Marie had the good sense to throw herself on her uncle's mercy. "I have no other thought," she wrote him, "but to conform in everything to your ideas and to follow absolutely everything that you command."

He packed her off to Italy. Shortly afterward, she

married Prince Colonna and embarked on the gay and dissolute life of a Roman matron.

Nothing in her afterlife touches the heart like that solitary vigil under the wide, slow-wheeling skies of the Charente. And some say that Louis never really loved anyone again as much as he did Marie.

Everywhere the Court went on their journey to the south, Louis was royally greeted. On the verge of peace, the country saw in him the living symbol of the good years to come.

On October 14, he made a state entry into Toulouse that was typical. There is a revealing painting of the event in one of the museums in that famous old city. Eight aldermen are kneeling before his carriage in their ermine-trimmed robes. The oldest and noblest is presenting the King with a book listing the privileges of the city. In the carriage window Louis, who is just twenty-two now, seems to embody all that is young and bursting with health. The Bourbon nose has been straightened by the artist and the Hapsburg lip made less full. The air of majesty is almost palpable.

Behind him is his mother in the black widow's dress she always wore. This time the artist has been less flattering: the nose droops, the Hapsburg lips sag. But the white horses drawing the carriage are splendid, and the whole scene is so fresh that it could have been painted the day before yesterday.

At Aix in January of 1660, Louis received the Great Condé. His errant cousin knelt before him, head bowed.

"I would like to buy back with the best part of my

blood all the trouble I have caused inside and outside France," he said humbly.

Louis helped him rise to his feet.

"My cousin, after your former great services to the Crown, I intend to forget actions which have harmed only yourself."

They talked of past campaigns in so pleasant a fashion that Condé felt as if it had all been done in Louis' service. Later he remarked that his pardon had been given with such pride that "it taught me that from now on I had a master." He never wavered again in his loyalty, and along with Turenne won many more victories for France.

The following June was the month agreed on for the wedding. By royal convention, Louis could not lay eyes on his bride until the day itself.

A few days before, his mother and her brother, King Philip IV of Spain, met for the first time in forty-six years. The reunion took place on the Île des Faisans. Its purpose was to confer on final arrangements for the wedding and to hear the articles of the Treaty of the Pyrenees read aloud. The Infanta Maria Theresa was also in the party.

Young Louis "happened" to be riding that morning along the French shore of the Bidassoa. He slipped into the wooden building on the island incognito.

Sitting beside the Infanta, Philip d'Anjou saw Maria Theresa glance at the doorway where his brother was standing.

"What does Your Majesty think of that—door?" he asked.

She laughed, knowing at once who it was who stood there.

"That door seems to me extremely beautiful and very nice," she said.

For his part, Louis had a good look at the blonde Princess so often painted by Velázquez. He was quite pleased with what he saw. Her hair was parted in a rather unfashionable way which left the brow bare, and she was rather short. But her skin was very white and her eyes were kind. She looked sweet and rather shy, which was exactly what she was.

Three days later they were married in the old stone church at Saint-Jean de Luz a few miles up the coast from the border. It was quite a scene, with Spanish fashion in marked contrast to French. Philip IV and his grandees were dressed in black velvet, with the magnificent Order of the Golden Fleece across their shoulders and chest. The Spanish nobles and their ladies all wore large white ruffs edged in lace. The ladies too were in black, and their dresses had very straight, low-cut bodices.

By contrast, the French looked like upstarts. Too many jewels and feathers, too much lace and finery. Even the elegant French swords lacked some of the dignity of the big, basket-hilted rapiers of the Spanish grandees.

It was, as one observer noted, the last victory of Spanish fashion, which had set the style in Europe for many years.

After the ceremony, Louis and Maria Theresa came out of the church by the door in the right transept. In honor of the event, the door was immediately walled up so that no one else would ever pass through.

The pair were married all over again in a civil ceremony at the Hôtel de Ville. Then, the following morning, with both Louis and Maria Theresa "in the gayest spirits," they started north on the last leg of the royal progress, reaching Paris in late August.

On their way north Louis slipped away for a night and went to Brouage. He knew that Marie Mancini had gone by now, but he slept in the bed that had been hers and mooned along the battlements—just as she had done, taking a last farewell.

Then, ready for what lay ahead, he rejoined the royal progress.

20. DEATH OF A CARDINAL

On August 26, 1660, the King and his new Queen made their triumphal entry into Paris. Near the famous Porte Saint-Antoine a throne had been constructed under a great arch, and here they received the keys of the capital city.

Then Louis mounted a Spanish barb, and the Queen climbed into a golden carriage. All the way to the Palais Royal they passed under triumphal arches. The streets were strewn with flowers and herbs, and as the carriage wheels crushed them, the air was filled with fragrance.

It was Cardinal Mazarin's hour of glory as well as that of the royal pair. But Mazarin was by now a very ill man—so riddled by gout and gallstones that he had to watch the procession from a balcony. Anne of Austria was as always by his side.

When the cavalcade reached the balcony Louis reined in his horse. He doffed his plumed hat and bowed low in the saddle. It was more than a gesture, it was a deeply felt tribute to the mother he loved and the minister who had created his now-peaceable kingdom.

Nearing sixty, exhausted by his work, Mazarin was soon a tragic husk of what he had once been.

"That man," said the Spanish Ambassador brutally as the Prime Minister tottered past one day, "bears a remarkable resemblance to the late Cardinal Mazarin."

Since his final return from exile, Mazarin had become richer than ever before. One estimate was that his income was the equivalent of a million dollars a year. His collection of sculpture and painting was among the finest in Europe, and he had even managed to reassemble most of the books that had been pillaged from his library.

He hated to die. There is a celebrated account of his last farewell to the treasures he had collected so passionately. It is from the *Mémoires* of Loménie de Brienne, and here it is in part:

> I heard him coming from the shuffling of his slippers which he dragged along the floor like a man who is very weak. I hid behind the tapestry and I heard him saying, "I must leave all that." He stopped and paused at every step because he was very feeble, turning first to one side and then to the other and casting his eyes upon the objects which appeared before him. . . . Turning around he added, "And also that. What terrible efforts it has cost me to acquire those things! Can I leave them? Can I abandon them without regret? . . . I shan't see them any more where I am going."

Toward the end, Mazarin retired to the castle of Vincennes. The Queen Mother hovered around his bed, driving him almost wild with her concern and her panic.

"This woman will be the death of me yet!" he cried.

Louis was with him often. At one point Mazarin told

him he wanted him to have all his vast possessions. Louis thought it over for a while. Finally, to Mazarin's relief, he refused, and the eight nieces shared the inheritance.

By tradition a French king could not be in the presence of death. So, as the end came near, Louis reluctantly took his leave.

"Sire, I owe you all," said Mazarin. "But I think I have evened matters by leaving you Colbert."

This was the young member of his staff who would one day become one of France's greatest public servants.

Mazarin died calmly and well, first receiving extreme unction in the full regalia of a Cardinal.

"Holy Virgin have pity on me and receive my soul," he said at the last.

When a devoted follower of the Cardinal's, the Marshal de Gramont, brought Louis the sad news, the King's comment was simple and touching. "Alas, M. le Maréchal, you and I have both lost a good friend."

The reaction of the French people was quite different. For all his achievements in bringing peace and security, their Italian Prime Minister was widely and cordially disliked.

Remembering Richelieu, one wit composed this epitaph:

"Here lies the second Eminence
—God keep us from a third!"

When one of Mazarin's doctors appeared in public, someone called out: "Gentlemen, a cheer! Here is the good doctor who killed the Cardinal!"

Long afterward, the historian Sainte-Beuve wrote that "the French could not have stood him one day more."

But Louis knew what his godfather had created and what lessons he himself had learned from him.

Soon, in a time of very great danger to his throne, he would have the chance to put Mazarin's teachings to the test.

21. "HOW HIGH WILL I NOT CLIMB?"

On March 10, 1661, the day after Cardinal Mazarin's death, Louis called the Royal Council together. His opening remarks to the eight officials present were brief and to the point:

> I have summoned you . . . to tell you that until now I have been quite willing to let my affairs be managed by the late Cardinal; in future I shall be my own Prime Minister.

To their amazement, he told them they could sign no dispatches, seal no agreements, pay out no money without his approval.

When, a few hours later, the Archbishop of Rouen—the presiding prelate of France—was granted an audience, the following exchange took place.

"Your Majesty ordered me to consult the late Cardinal on all matters," the Archbishop said. "To whom does Your Majesty wish I should address myself in future?"

"To me."

One day he was discussing a certain minor item with the Portuguese Ambassador.

"I will settle this matter with Your Majesty's ministers," said the diplomat.

"I have no ministers," said Louis. "You mean to say my men of business."

Despite such evidence that he really meant to take over, many thought that this wish to rule was just a whim, and that he would soon revert to the pursuit of pleasure.

The man who was most convinced of this was Nicolas Fouquet, the brilliant and devious Superintendent of Finance. Fouquet, now forty-four, was sure that he would be the next Prime Minister. During the Fronde he had been faithful to Mazarin, and he had reason to believe that he still stood well with the Queen Mother. Again and again, by clever manipulations, he had produced enough money to make the Cardinal's ambitious plans possible.

He was a man whose great charm matched his great ambition. He had lean, rather delicate features and the hands of an artist. The long-lashed eyes held an intensity that was both compelling and disturbing.

He came from a modest Breton family of six sons and six daughters. By his own skills he had made himself the richest and most powerful man in the kingdom. His crest was a squirrel, and the motto was *Quo Non Ascendam?* or *How high will I not climb?*

It was a good question. Fouquet already had a private army and navy of his own. Just to be safe, he had bought a ten-mile-long rocky island called Belle-Île, off the southern coast of Brittany, and put some fifteen hundred men to work fortifying it. He was Marquis de Belle-Île, Vicomte de Melun and Vaux, viceroy of the New World. He was a patron of all the arts, a philosopher, historian, geographer, scientist.

A courtier of the time remarked that Fouquet would have been the perfect man if he could ever have gotten buildings and women out of his mind.

His love of architecture was almost as overwhelming as his love of women. In 1656 he started to build Vaux-le-Vicomte, the castle southeast of Paris that would become one of the wonders of its time.

Fouquet commissioned three men of promise to work together—Le Vau, Le Brun, and Le Nôtre—architect, artist, and landscape gardener. What they produced, in harmony and grandeur, can still be seen. Vaux-le-Vicomte sits on a stone platform presiding over 170 acres of gardens and pools, canals and yew hedges, all in perfect symmetry. With its steep slate roofs, its fine dome supported by sixteen marble arches, its two immense pavilioned wings, the château itself has a style and a scale that is the noble essence of a whole century.

Inside, the ceilings and murals painted in Le Brun's rich, elegant style, still dazzle and delight. Around the high golden cornices of the State rooms there is a mischievous little chorus of squirrels peering down, as if to remind the viewer how high they have already climbed.

Vaux-le-Vicomte took four years to build and cost the staggering sum of fifteen million livres.

There was something nervous and a little squirrel-like about Nicolas Fouquet himself. Now, with everything seeming to go his way, and his great pleasure dome complete at last, his sharp ears picked up a sound of danger in the wind. Even though he saw the King every day, and Louis was invariably polite and appreciative of his services, some chafing unease remained.

To cover himself, Fouquet confessed to the King that he had practiced certain financial irregularities during the time of Mazarin. Louis waved this aside as something over and past, and the Superintendent, much relieved, promised there would be no more cutting of corners.

What Fouquet did not know was that Mazarin, dying, had warned the King against Fouquet's ambition. At the same time, he had recommended a fuller use of Colbert's more solid virtues.

Louis made Colbert Assistant Superintendent of Finance, directly under Fouquet. So Colbert was now in a perfect position to observe and report on the labyrinthine activities of his superior, whom he cordially hated.

Fouquet's greed knew no limits. He loaned himself money at a high rate of interest, faked the expense sheets, reported income as lower than it was.

By great perseverance, Colbert discovered all this and told the King. Louis gave Fouquet chance after chance to regularize the accounts, but he never did. He had grown so arrogant, so sure that the system was too complicated for anyone but himself to unravel, that he plunged recklessly on.

By May 1661, Louis had made up his mind that Fouquet must go. Was he already too powerful to pull down? Louis might have had him quietly killed, but he was not a cruel man—and what if an attempt failed?

He decided to watch and wait—the game he had learned so well from Mazarin.

During that summer Maria Theresa was with child. Although Louis continued to treat her with the exquisite courtesy that was so deep a part of his nature, he was beginning to be bored with the bride that had been forced on him. Her French never did improve much, her mind was shapeless and superstitious. Years later, when she died, Louis said, "The only time she ever caused me suffering was when she left me." This was graceful, and in character. But in the meantime the monarch was in the mood to look around for someone a little more mettlesome.

First his favorite companion was his own sister-in-law, Henrietta of England. The "skinny little girl" was now married to Philip d'Anjou. She was so pretty and witty and gay that half the Court was in love with her.

Finding that she and Louis were getting themselves talked about, and not wishing to hurt Maria Theresa's feelings, Anne of Austria suggested to Louis that he pretend to shift his attentions to one of Henrietta's ladies-in-waiting.

Louis thought this an amusing idea, and picked out Louise de la Vallière. She was a country girl from the Touraine, with blue eyes and ash-blonde hair. Unlike Marie Mancini and Henrietta, who were girls with a good deal of self-assurance, Louise had an appealing shyness and gentleness. Although she walked with a slight limp, she rode like a streak, even bareback.

Soon they were inseparable. At Fontainebleau, during the warm, magic summer of 1661, they were rarely apart.

The old palace was full of the memories of other royal lovers. In the gleaming ballroom of Henry II, Henry's initials and those of Diane de Poitiers were entwined for all the world to see. Down the long galleries and the glades of the pleasant forest, Louis' own grandfather, Henry of Navarre, had often strolled with his beloved Gabrielle d'Estrées, in an idyll that seemed to have no end.

Soon, true to this very French tradition of dynastic wives and enchanting mistresses, Louis and Louise became lovers.

None of this was lost on Fouquet, who had his spies at Court. Now he made a mistake. He tried to bribe Louise to speak well of him to the King. Louise told Louis, and Louis was furious.

Then he made another mistake. He went to Anne of Austria and accused her of ingratitude after all he had done in the bad time of the Fronde and after. He quite forgot that he was a commoner talking to a queen, and a proud Spanish one at that. She dismissed him very curtly indeed.

On the surface all was still serene. He was the most powerful man in the kingdom, with the ear of the King, any number of women friends, a fleet of his own, a private army, an island retreat in case of trouble, and one of the finest palaces in Europe. To all appearances he was the happiest of men.

He decided to have a party, to convince others—and himself—how wonderfully happy he was.

22. SUPPER CHEZ FOUQUET

It was one of the most famous parties of all time. The date was August 17, 1661. Six thousand guests sat down to supper on the terrace of Vaux-le-Vicomte. They dined off gold and silver plates, the gold being for the royal family and the Princes of the Blood. The lesser lords and the bourgeoisie were served on silver.

The chef was the incomparable Vatel, who later went to work for the Great Condé (and killed himself during another royal occasion when there wasn't enough roast to go around).

Molière presented a new play and La Fontaine read a poem in honor of the evening. At one point a large artificial whale was drawn through the canal, spouting fire. When the King made the tour of the gardens, the fountains were so boisterous it seemed as if he were walking between walls of water.

Louis drove over from Fontainebleau in a two-wheeled calèche with the top down. Louise de la Vallière and the Comtesse de Guiche kept him company, with the Queen Mother following in her own coach. Their escort was a regiment of musketeers, commanded by M. d'Artagnan—the sturdy Gascon who inspired Dumas' immortal character.

They arrived at six in the evening.

Fouquet and his wife met the royal party in the courtyard. The superintendent almost prostrated himself on the cobblestones in his pleasure (and relief). After Louis and his mother had each taken a short rest, he showed them the State apartments.

In the dining room was a fine portrait of Louis by Le Brun, which the King did not even know had been painted. He admired it in his courteous way.

"It's yours," said Fouquet airily.

In the grand salon the whole ceiling was a blazing sun in saffron, crimson, and scarlet. For the moment Louis was gratified that his own emblem was so symbolically used.

Fouquet, who was walking just behind the King, stepped forward and asked permission to explain the allegory.

"Pray do so," said Louis.

"The sun—the center of the universe, the creator of light and heat and life—is your Majesty. Deprived of your gracious presence, we sink into darkness and death. That star beside the sun is myself, sire, receiving light from your benignant rays."

Louis saw that the star was very close to the sun. He frowned in displeasure and moved on. But Fouquet was too busy showing off his own grandeur to notice.

In another room, there was a mural of Fidelity, escorted by Prudence and Reason.

"I am told that Fidelity represents Fouquet himself, your Majesty," the Duc de Saint-Aignan, who was in attendance, whispered to the King.

"What on earth can Fidelity have to do with a superintendent of finance?" Louis whispered back. Then, raising his voice:

"Let us leave this room—it stifles me."

The tour of the gardens revealed more wonders. Every tree and plant was illuminated so cleverly that the whole garden seemed one great blazing carpet. Beyond the formal patterns of the garden *à la français*, long vistas of oak and lime stretched away, so skillfully lit that they seemed like vaults of fire. The splendid façade of the castle was outlined by clusters of golden lamps.

Several military bands on the high terrace took turns in cheerful rivalry with the soft strains of violin and lute from the gardens below.

After supper Molière presented his new farce called *Les Fâcheux*, which gave the King great pleasure.

During the presentation, one of Louis' courtiers whispered to him something that gave him no pleasure at all: in a remote part of his castle, Fouquet had a private gallery full of paintings of beautiful women he had known. Among them was a portrait of Louise de la Vallière.

Louis' temper flared up several more times that night. As a man of taste, he could not help admiring the magnificence of Vaux and the skill with which the fête was staged. But now he knew by the evidence of his own eyes and ears that Fouquet had created a kingdom of his own within the kingdom of France. He was far more royal than the King! And his great golden palace of brick and stone and marble was all built with money stolen from the royal treasury.

During the tour of the gardens, Louis communicated his growing anger to his mother.

"Madame," he murmured, "shall we make these people disgorge?"

And again, later in the evening:

"Let's leave now! I can't stand it here another minute."

She tried to calm him.

"I'd like to have M. Fouquet arrested on the spot," he muttered.

"That would scarcely be to your honor," Anne answered. "Everyone can see that this poor man is ruining himself to give you good cheer. You can't arrest him in his own house!"

Louis' self-control came back, and he managed to appear both agreeable and urbane as the evening went on.

At its climax the great dome began to glow. Then it seemed to explode into flame like a volcano, as the last set piece of fireworks went the sky.

When Louis' calèche finally rolled away in the small hours, Fouquet was a happy man. He was sure that his future was safe, and that the post of Prime Minister was within his reach at last.

23. THE FALL OF THE SQUIRREL

Some French historians say that Fouquet's fate was decided on that night at Vaux. The news that he had hung a portrait of Louise de la Vallière in his gallery of fair women is supposed to have triggered the King's revenge.

In fact, Louise was quickly able to convince Louis that Fouquet meant nothing to her and never had. Moreover we know from Louis' own very precise memoirs that the removal and disgrace of his high-flying squirrel of a superintendent had been determined at least three months before the fête.

The King laid his plans skillfully and well. They combined the bold and the artful in a way that Mazarin would have approved.

Among Fouquet's offices was that of attorney general, which carried with it membership in the Paris Parlement. Members could only be brought to trial before the Parlement itself. So the first step was to isolate him from this close-knit body.

Through Colbert, Louis suggested to Fouquet that he might want to relinquish his attorney generalship. The clear implication was that by doing this he would make himself more eligible than ever to be Prime Minister.

Fouquet tumbled into the trap. He sold the post for fourteen hundred thousand livres, of which he turned over a full million to the King for his own urgent needs.

Louis was not unhappy to have the money, which he needed badly. But the insolence of the gesture was something else again. Fouquet seemed to think he could even bribe the King!

Anyway, Louis was now free to move with less fear that the Superintendent would be protected by the Parlement.

In late August the Court moved to Nantes, the ancient capital of Brittany near the mouth of the Loire. The King planned to hold an assembly there to meet with his Breton subjects.

Fouquet reached Nantes ahead of his master. He was feeling a little easier in his mind because his own stronghold of Belle-Île, his army and fleet, were all within easy reach.

By now he was like a man with undulant fever. Hot ambition alternated with cold fear. He was too clever not to sense that something was in the air, and he was quite aware that the dour Colbert was his mortal enemy. But he was so vain and reckless that his faith in his own destiny always came surging back after the periods of misgiving.

On September 1, Louis summoned his friend D'Artagnan to the royal chambers in the old castle at Nantes. He knew that the Gascon musketeer was on good terms with Fouquet, but he liked and trusted him nonetheless.

D'Artagnan begged to be excused, saying he was in bed with a high fever. Louis summoned him again. D'Artagnan came and stood before the King. He trembled so with his fever that Louis took pity on him and told him to go back to bed.

"Get well as quickly as you can, M. D'Artagnan," he said. "I have a most important mission to entrust to you."

Good soldier that he was, D'Artagnan made a quick recovery. Three days later he was called to the King's study. There, in deep secrecy, Louis told him that he had decided to arrest the mighty Superintendent of Finance. The musketeer was given meticulous instructions. Finally, when Louis dismissed him, he received his written orders.

Back in his own quarters, D'Artagnan read and reread them until the incredible fact was etched on his mind:

> His Majesty has ordered and orders the Sieur d'Artagnan of the company of his mounted musketeers to arrest the said Sieur Fouquet and to conduct him under good and certain guard . . . to the place mentioned.

It was announced that the King would hunt the next day, right after the morning meeting of the Council. This meant that D'Artagnan could have a troop of musketeers in the castle courtyard—and a royal carriage ready to spirit Fouquet away—without causing any alarm.

Perfect timing and the luck of the bold would still be necessary. Failure, the King reminded D'Artagnan, could only lead to another Fronde, more bitter than any that had gone before.

On the morning of September 5, at seven o'clock, the Royal Council met. Late the evening before, Fouquet had received a note from a friend warning him to escape while he could: *Send your sedan chair with the curtains drawn, but empty, to the castle and leave town by another route.* But he was in one of his rising moods of hope and confidence, with his "triumph" at Vaux still very fresh in his mind. He was one of the first at the morning meeting.

The King made it clear that he was in a hurry to go hunting. Little new business was brought up. When, within fifteen minutes, Louis adjourned the Council, Colbert and the three other members who were present filed out quickly.

Louis signaled Fouquet to stay behind.

The King pretended to search for a paper on his document-strewn table by the window of the room. Actually he was looking down into the courtyard to make sure that D'Artagnan's men were properly posted there. He saw the Gascon and a score or so of his musketeers strolling about on foot, and knew that all was going according to plan.

Then he dismissed Fouquet with every mark of friendship. The Superintendent bowed low and long, backing all the way to the door as he did so.

Outside the Council Chamber, the great staircase of the castle was thronged with people who wanted to ask favors of the great Fouquet. He chatted awhile, enjoying as always the feeling of power, then started to move through the crowd toward the main gateway.

And disappeared.

D'Artagnan had of course placed another squad of men outside this western gate, which was on the other side of the castle from the court. But the crowd was so dense that Fouquet had apparently slipped through and away.

D'Artagnan sent a message to the King saying he feared he had failed, and asking for orders. Louis went into one of his rare rages but sent back no positive ideas what to do next.

Suddenly Fouquet was seen again. He emerged from the throng before the castle, calling for his sedan chair. When it came, he climbed in and headed for the cathedral square.

It was there that D'Artagnan and a squad of musketeers caught up with him, still surrounded by a lot of hangers-on and petitioners. Saying that he had an urgent message, the musketeer shouldered his way through.

Fouquet climbed out of his chair and started to raise his hat in salutation.

"Monsieur," said D'Artagnan, "I arrest you by the King's orders!"

Fouquet's hand fell to his side, and he turned very pale. He asked to see the warrant and read it several times over.

"I thought I stood higher with the King than anyone in France," he said, half to himself.

He seemed anxious to avoid any tumult. D'Artagnan suggested that they step into one of the houses on the square.

Once inside, D'Artagnan searched his prisoner. During this humiliating business, Fouquet talked away with great assurance, all his charm and confidence returning.

Shortly afterward, one of the King's carriages came up at the trot, escorted by four mounted musketeers in their blue, silver-crossed cassocks. Fouquet and D'Artagnan climbed quickly in, and they rolled away.

At a nearby village they picked up an escort of a hundred cavalrymen. Two nights later the cavalcade reached the grim, many-turreted castle of Angers on the Loire. It had been chosen as the temporary pretrial prison for the man who had climbed too high.

He would never breathe free air again.

That night Louis wrote an exultant letter to his mother, describing in vivid detail how Fouquet nearly slipped away and how D'Artagnan "caught him again in the place where the great church stands."

Then the letter struck a note that would recur often during his long reign: "I have told those gentlemen who are with me that I would have no more superintendents, but myself take the work of finance . . . knowing that this is the true way to place myself in affluence and relieve my people."

Later, in his *Instructions to the Dauphin*, Louis told his son (born that same year) what it had been like to discover his own powers at this anxious time: "I felt myself rising as it were both in mind and courage; I found in myself what I had no idea of, and I joyfully reproached myself for having been so long ignorant of it. Then it dawned on me that I was King, and was born to be."

This confidence of his, so long forming, would carry him through all the years—the brilliant and gaudy and war-scarred years, the glorious and ultimately tragic years—that lay head.

Young Louis was his own man at last.

EPILOGUE

"Disorder reigned everywhere," Louis XIV wrote in his memoirs, describing the time when he took over. This was somewhat of an exaggeration, although government housecleaning was certainly overdue. In matters of finance and justice there was incredible corruption. The nobles were restless, the peasants near-starving. But there did exist peace in Europe for as long as Louis wished to keep it. France was ready for a firm hand, and he was strong and ready to use one.

"Louis XIV had nothing more than good sense, but he had a great deal of it," Sainte-Beuve once wrote. It is one of those vast simplifications that the famous historian was so fond of making.

No man ever worked harder at what Louis himself called the *métier de roi*—the profession of king. He proved to be a born leader of men, with a wonderful eye for spotting talent. And he had the greater gift of making men in many fields do better than their best.

Colbert, Louvois, Bossuet, Pascal, La Fontaine, Molière, Racine, Le Brun, Le Vaux, Le Nôtre, Condé, Turenne,

Vauban—these are a few of the men of his era who now belong to all time.

Art, architecture, sculpture, music, science, theology, war, finance, justice were among the fields of their excellence. No wonder the years from 1661, when this story closes, and 1715, when Louis died, came to be known as the Splendid Century and the Age of Louis XIV.

There is a darker side to the golden coin. Louis was a man who outlived his time. His love of war became an obsession for war. That fine natural courtesy of his froze into empty protocol. His simple Catholic faith turned intolerant. He became impaled on his own power and glory.

It is best to leave him at a time when he stood revealed in the clear light of noon—a time of vigor unimpaired and promise fulfilled.

CHRONOLOGY

1638	September 5, birth of the future Louis XIV at Saint-Germain.
1642	December 4, death of Cardinal Richelieu.
1643	May 14, Louis XIV inherits the throne on the death of his father, Louis XIII.
	May 18, Cardinal Mazarin becomes prime minister.
	May 19, the battle of Rocroi, French victory over the Hapsburgs.
1648	August 2, the battle of Lens.
	August 28, the arrest of Counselor Broussel starts the period of civil war known as the Fronde (1648–52).
	Octotber 24, the Treaty of Westphalia ends the Thirty Years' War.
1649	January 5, Louis XIV escapes from Paris by night.
1650	January 18, arrest of the Great Condé.
1651	February 19, the Paris mob storms the Palais Royal to see Louis XIV.
	September 5–7, Louis XIV's ceremonial coming-of-age.
1652	April 6, the battle of Bléneau.
	July 2, the Great Mademoiselle turns the cannon of the Bastille on the royal troops.
	October 21, Louis XIV reenters Paris.
1654	June 6, coronation of Louis XIV at Reims.
1658	June 15, the Battle of the Dunes.
1659	During the spring, Louis XIV and Marie Mancini fall hopelessly in love.
	November 7, the Treaty of the Pyrenees is signed by France and Spain.
1660	June, marriage festivities of Louis XIV and Infanta Maria Theresa.
1661	March 9, death of Cardinal Mazarin.
	August - 17, Superintendent Fouquet's six-thousand-guest party at Vaux-le-Vicomte.
	September 5, Louis XIV arrests Fouquet and begins to rule in his own right.

BIBLIOGRAPHY

In English:

BLUNT, ANTHONY. *Art and Architecture in France, 1500–1700.* Baltimore: Penguin Books, 1954.

CRONIN, VINCENT. *Louis XIV.* Boston: Houghton Mifflin Company, 1965.

DE GRAMONT, SANCHE. *Epitaph for Kings.* New York: G. P. Putnam's Sons, 1967.

DE RETZ, CARDINAL. *Memoirs.* Historic Court Memoirs, No. 6. New York: Grolier Society, n.d.

DURANT, WILL and ARIEL. *The Age of Louis XIV.* Story of Civilization, vol. 8. New York: Simon & Schuster, 1963.

ERLANGER, PHILIPPE. *The Age of Courts and Kings.* New York: Harper & Row, 1967.

GUIZOT, M. *A Popular History of France.* Boston: Dana Estes and Charles E. Lauriat, n.d.

HALL, GEOFFREY, and SANDERS, JOAN. *D'Artagnan, The Ultimate Musketeer.* Boston: Houghton Mifflin Company, 1964.

LEWIS, W. H. *Assault on Olympus.* New York: Harcourt, Brace & Company, 1958.

LEWIS, W. H. *The Splendid Century, Life in the France of Louis XIV.* New York: William Sloane Associates, 1954.

SAINTE-BEUVE, C. A. *Portraits of the Seventeenth Century.*

Translated by Katherine P. Wormeley. New York: Frederick Ungar, 1964.

SEDGWICK, HENRY DWIGHT. *France, A Short History*. Boston: Little, Brown & Company, 1929.

STEEGMÜLLER, FRANCIS. *The Grand Mademoiselle*. New York: Farrar, Straus & Cudahy, 1956.

TAYLOR, FRANCIS HENRY. *The Taste of Angels*. Boston: (Atlantic Monthly Press) Little, Brown & Company, 1948.

WOLF, JOHN B. *Louis XIV*. New York: W. W. Norton & Company, 1968.

In French:

BOULLET, LUCIEN. *Histoire de Rocroi*. Mezières: Editions de la Société d'Etudes Ardennaises, 1958.

ERLANGER, PHILIPPE. *Louis XIV*. Paris: Fayard, Les Grandes Etudes Historiques, 1965.

FANIEL, STEPHANE, directeur. *Le XVIIe Siècle Français*. Collection Connaissance des Arts. Paris: Hachette, 1958.

LORRIS, PIERRE-GEORGES. *Le Cardinal de Retz*. Paris: Albin Michel, 1956.

Louis XIV, par lui-même. Edited by Michel Déon. Paris: Librairie Académique Perrin, 1964.

METTRA, CLAUDE. *Les Bourbons*. Tome I. Lausanne: Editions Rencontre, 1968.

MONGRÉDIEN, GEORGES, directeur. *Mazarin*. Collection Génies et Réalités. Paris: Hachette, 1959.

POISSON, GEORGE. *Promenades aux châteaux de l'Ile-de-France*. Paris: André Balland, 1967.

TOUDOUZE, GUSTAVE. *Le Roy Soleil*. Illustrated by Maurice Leloir. Paris: Combet & Cie., 1904.

INDEX

Anne of Austria: attempts of, to find royal bride, 107, 108, 109; correspondence from Mazarin to, 71–72; and Day of the Barricades, 47, 50, 51, 52; described, 7, 25–26; and Fronde of the Princes, 66, 67–68, 75, 77; gives birth to Louis, 3–4; and Louis XIII, 6, 12; and Louis XIV, 105–107, 133; lovers of, 22; and Mazarin, 24–25, 26; named Regent, 35; and Parlement, 38–39; plots against Louis and Marie, 110; relinquishes power as Regent, 74. *See also* Court

d'Artagnan, arrests Nicolas Fouquet, 135–138

d'Artois, Comte, 27

Beauvais, Bishop of, 91

Bidassoa River, 111

Bléneau, battle of, 78–79

Bouillon, Duc de, 40, 77

Bourbon, Duc Louis Henri de, Prince de Condé (the Great Condé), 86, 96, 113; arrested, 64; attempts to capture Paris, 81–84; attempts to seize power, 85; at battle of Bléneau, 77–79; at Battle of the Dunes, 101–102; at battle of Lens, 41; at battle of Rocroi, 17–21; commands Frondeurs at Paris, 83–85; demands on, by Fronde of the Princes, 62–64; freed by Mazarin, 69; at Fribourg, 40; and the Fronde, 58; at Lérida, 40; and Louis XIV, 70–71; and Mazarin, 62; pardoned by Louis XIV, 115–116; returns to Paris, 70; siege of Paris, 59–60; as soldier, 16–17

Brienne, Lomenie de, courtier, 65–66; *Mémoires* quoted, 120

Britte, Don Antonio, governor of Lérida, 40

Brouage, France, 114

Broussel, Counselor: arrested, 47; released, 52

Buckingham, Duke of, 22

Charlemagne, crown of, 93–95

Clovis I, king of the Franks, 88–91

Comminges, officer of Anne of Austria, 47
Condé, the Great. *See* Bourbon, Duc Louis Henri de, Prince de Condé
Conti, Prince de, 58; arrested, 64, freed by Mazarin, 69
coronation, ceremony of, 90
Court: escapes from Paris, 53–55; returns to Paris, 60; at Saint-Germain, 55–57
Cromwell, Oliver, 101

dauphin, origin of term, 4
Day of the Barricades. *See* Paris
Dunes, Battle of the, 101–102
Dunkirk. *See* Dunes, Battle of the

Erlanger, Philippe, quoted, 49

Fouquet, Nicolas, 99, 128; described, 124–125; fall and arrest of, 135–139; and Louis XIV, 126, 129–132, 133–139; party of, at Vaux-le-Vicomte, 129–133
Fribourg, 40
Fronde, the, 45–46, 52, 53, 57–60, 88
Fronde of the Princes, 65–70, 74–86
Frontenac, Comtesse de, 105
Fuentès, Count of, 19–21

Hapsburg dynasty, 16, 53
Haro, Don Luis de, negotiates Treaty of Pyrenees, 111–113
Henrietta of England, 127
d'Hocquincourt, Marshal, 77, 78
l'Hôpital, Marshal de, 17

Île des Faisans, 111

Instructions to the Dauphin, quoted, 139

Jarzé, Marquis de, 64
"la Joyeuse," sword of Louis XIV, 92–93

La Fontaine, Jean de, 129
La Meilleraye, Marshal de, 50, 51
Lansac, Marquise de, 4, 5
La Porte, valet to young Louis XIV, 27, 28–29
La Rochefoucauld, Duc François de, 58–59, 83, 86; *Maximes* quoted, 60
La Vallière, Louise de, and Louis XIV, 127, 128
Le Brun, Charles, 125
Le Nôtre, André, 125
Lens, battle of, 41
Leopold William, Archduke, 41
Lérida, Spain, 40
Le Vau, Louis, 125
lits de justice, 35–36, 38–39
Longueville, Duc de, 64, 69
Longueville, Duchesse de, 58, 59
Louis XIII: and Anne of Austria, 6, 12; attempts to create regency, 12–13; decline and death of, 11–14; described, 6–7, 10; and Louis XIV, 7–8, 9; prophesy on battle of Rocroi, 13; and Richelieu, 11; at son's birth, 3–4, 5; wish of, for regency council thwarted, 36
Louis XIV: and Anne of Austria, 26, 105–107; birth of, 3–4; ceremony of coming of age of, 72–75; childhood passion for war, 15; and Condé, 70–71; contracts typhoid, 102–104; coronation of, at Reims, 91–

95; and Fronde of the Princes, 65–66, 67–68, 77; and Henrietta of England, 127; and La Porte, 29; in *lit de justice*, 35–36; and Louis XIII, 7–8, 9; and Louise de la Vallière, 127, 128; loves of, 105–107; and Maria Theresa, 127; and Marie Mancini, 104, 107, 108, 109–110, 113, 114; marriage of, to Maria Theresa, 117–118; and Mazarin, 29–30, 98, 103, 113, 120–121; near death at age nine, 30–32; and Nicolas Fouquet, 126, 129–132, 133–139; pardons Condé, 115–116; and Parlement, 99–100; as public performer, 99; reenters Paris, 85–86; reign of, evaluated, 140–141; and Royal Council, 123; as soldier, 97; state entry of, into Toulouse, 115. *See also* Court

Mancini, Marie, 114–115; described, 104–105; and Louis XIV, 104, 107, 108, 109–110, 113, 114
Maria Theresa, Infanta of Spain, 116–117, 127; marriage of, to Louis XIV, 117–118
Mazarin, Jules (Giulio Mazarini): and Anne of Austria, 24–25, 26; attacks on, 57–58; attempts of, to secure royal bride, 107, 109; career of, 22–23; and Condé, 62; and Day of the Barricades, 50; decline and death of, 119–121; exile correspondence of, with Anne of Austria, 71–72; flees Paris, 70; frees the three Princes, 69; and the Fronde, 45, 49, 53; and Fronde of the Princes, 66–67; and Louis XIV, 29–30, 98, 103, 113; named Prime Minister, 36; negotiates Treaty of Pyrenees, 111–113; and Parlement, 37–38, 41–42; plots to separate Louis and Marie, 110; public reaction to death of, 121–122; return of, 77; and Richelieu, 23–24; temporary exile of, 85. *See also* Court
"Mazarinades," quoted, 57
"Mazarinettes," 104
Melo, Don Francisco de, in battle of Rocroi, 16, 17–21
Molé, president of Parlement, 66
Molière, Jean Baptiste Poquelin, 129
Motteville, Madame de, 54; quoted, 32, 46, 104–105

Nantes, France, 135

Orleans, Anne Marie-Louise d', Duchesse de Montpensier, 34, 57; and Fronde of the Princes, 80, 81–82, 83, 84–85; orders Bastille cannons fired, 84–85; quoted, 56
Orleans, Gaston d', 3, 30–32, 70; character of, 33–34; and Fronde of the Princes, 81; joins Fronde, 65. *See also* Court

Paris: Court escapes from, 53–55; Court returns to, 60; Day of the Barricades, 47, 50–51; entry into, of Louis XIV and Queen Maria Theresa, 119; under siege by Condé, 59–60. *See also* Fronde

Parlement of Paris: and Anne of Austria, 38–39; and Court, 37; and Louis XIV, 99–100; and Mazarin, 41–42; political role of, 34–35. *See also* Fronde
Philip, Duc d'Anjou, 8. *See also* Court
Philip IV, King of Spain, 53
Pyrenees, Treaty of, 111–113

Reims, 88; coronation of Louis XIV at, 91–95
Retz, Cardinal de, Jean François Paul de Gondi, 47–49, 85; arrested, 86; and Day of the Barricades, 50–51, 52; and the Fronde, 58; and the Fronde of the Princes, 67, 77; *Mémoires* quoted, 34, 36, 49, 86
Richelieu, Duc de, Armand Jean du Plessis, 10–11
Rocroi, battle of, 13, 17–21
Rouen, Archbishop of, 123–124
Royal Council, and Louis XIV, 123

Sainte-Beuve, Charles Augustin, quoted, 122, 140
Saint-Germain, Court at, 55–57
Savoy, Princess Margaret of, 107–108
Séguier, Chancellor, 35
Senneterre, cavalryman at battle of Rocroi, 18
Soissons, Bishop of, at coronation of Louis XIV, 92–93, 95

Talon, Omer, on taxation at *lits de justice*, 38–39
taxation, excesses of, under Mazarin, 37
Thirty Years' War, 16, 52–53
Toulouse, France, 115
Turenne, Vicomte de, Henri de la Tour d'Auvergne, 40–41, 59, 77; at battle of Bléneau, 77–79; in Battle of the Dunes, 101–102; commands royal forces at Paris, 82–85; joins Fronde, 65

Vatel, French chef, 129
Vauban, Sébastien, French military engineer, 97–98
Vaux-le-Vicomte, 125; Fouquet's party at, 129–133
Villeroy, Marshal de, 54

Westphalia, Treaty of. *See* Thirty Years' War